INTRODUCING INFERENCE

Marilyn M. Toomey

illustrated by

Will Harney

CIRCUIT PUBLICATIONS

Marblehead, MA

04 03 02 01 00 TS 6 5 4 3 2 1

ISBN: 0-923573-44-5

TABLE OF CONTENTS

INTRODUCTION

Inference is a fundamental process that envelops much of our thinking. Guessing, implying, hinting, suggesting, supposing and reasoning are just a few mental processes in which we draw inference. Our ability to infer or to draw conclusions given only some of the necessary information is a cornerstone of our reasoning process. We use inference in our daily lives as well as in academic and professional areas. Often we must explain this process as we explain our reasons or defend our position on a topic. We recognize other people trying to explain their inferential reasoning when we hear it. Inferring is not a conscious process, yet it is pervasive in our thinking and in our communication.

It is important to be able to use this skill and to explain our inferences to others. So many factors in society and in education today require us to do this and to do it well. Our outcome-based efforts in educational, financial, technical and medical fields are obvious. We can help give our language students a greater chance of success in many important educational and, ultimately, professional areas if we help them approach inference more comfortably. To do this we must show them ways to use inference as they solve problems and figure out solutions. We must also guide students to use the *language* associated with inferential reasoning.

The purpose of this book is to help make inference more friendly and helpful to students. Students are shown a way to use inference in reasoning or in problem solving by recognizing that some information is missing and that more information is needed in order to solve a problem.

When we use inference:

1. We consider information that is given.

2. We identify information that is missing. This information is usually found in our own store of knowledge or experience.

3. We combine the information given and the information that we have supplied.

This is how we "figure things out." For example, if a child comes home crying with a scrape on her knee, her dad will infer that she has fallen down onto a rough surface and scraped her knee.

Here's what he did to figure this out:

1. Dad could see that the child's knee was scraped and was bleeding. He could see the child crying. (This information was given.)

2. He knows that falling down on a rough surface such as a sidewalk and scraping your knee can cause your knee to be bruised and to bleed. This could hurt badly enough to cause a child to cry. (He remembers falling and scraping his own knees as a little boy. He remembers how much this had hurt and that he cried.)

3. He concludes that the little girl fell down on a rough surface such as a sidewalk, and scraped her knee, and she was hurt badly enough to cause her to cry.

Throughout the book students will be encouraged not only to draw conclusions using inference. They will *tell how* they came to their conclusions. For language students *explaining* their reasons is often more difficult than solving problems. The book will teach students that using inference in their reasoning process is using their best *judgement*.

Most important of all, students should understand that they are super stars for figuring things out--not failures for inferring incorrectly. From the simplest tasks in the first part of the book to the last page, students should be praised for "good detective work" as they solve the problems and explain their reasons. They should be encouraged to understand that indentifying missing information in a written sentence or groups of sentences in many ways is like identifying missing parts of objects shown in pictures.

In the first part of the book students will identify missing parts of objects, animals, or sequenced events. They will be asked to tell about a part of an object, animal or sequence that is not shown. They will say how the item is supposed to look and how the pictured item is, therefore, incorrect. In later activities students will identify missing parts of sequenced events or processes shown in pictures. They will tell what part of the sequence or process is missing. Finally, they will predict or analyze outcomes, identifying and supplying different types of missing information. More detailed information about activities in Parts One and Two will be presented on pages directly preceding each part.

Will and I hope that this book helps you to introduce inference to your students in a way that is satisfying to you and enjoyable to your students.

In Part One students begin their introduction to inference by looking at pictures of people, animals or objects and identifying something that is obviously missing. From there they look for missing information in sequenced events presented in pictures. Finally, students must read or listen to a simple scenario and think about what is given and what is missing.

Aside from teaching students to associate inference tasks with identifying missing information, an important goal of this book is to encourage success and self-confidence in such tasks. The activities presented early in Part One (pages 2–13) present very simple questions with very obvious answers. If students are introduced to the notion of inference in such a friendly way they should be more comfortable when they must draw inferences in order to solve problems. In these early activities it is important to commend students who identify what is missing. Use every opportunity to praise their "good thinking" or good "detective work." Remind students that they knew what was missing because they knew what the subject was supposed to look like.

Pages 14–25 present sequences of three events, the third event showing the outcome of the two preceding events. Following this, pages 26–31 repeat each of these sequences, omitting the middle event. Here students must look at the initial event and the outcome and recall what had happened in between.

Pages 32–37 ask students what is probably going to happen at the end of a three-part sequence, the first two parts given. Here you introduce the important notion and language of *probability*. Students are asked to make a "good guess" as to what will happen. Developing the concept of probability is essential in building students' ability to draw inference.

Pages 38–43 present three-part sequences, the first and third part in place. Students must identify the middle part of each sequence by choosing the correct picture from random pictures shown at the bottom of the page. They are then asked to cut and paste the correct picture in the middle of the sequence. Following this (pages 44–47) students are shown the first and last part of a three-part sequence and asked what probably happened in between. In these tasks no picture clues are given. Students must fill in the missing information from their own knowledge and experience.

Pages 48–54 present a single picture showing the outcome of events along with questions leading a student to state his or her opinion about what probably happened to lead to this outcome.

Finally, pages 55–60 present simple scenarios and call upon students' ability to draw inferences as they tell "what probably happened." Activities on these pages offer a transition from simpler tasks using pictures to activities where a student must listen to or read a statement, then answer a question requiring inferential reasoning.

Throughout all of the activities in this part of the book you are strongly encouraged to ask your students *why* they answered the questions as they did. Understanding and telling how and why problems are solved as they are is sometimes more important than the solutions themselves. Our language students need all the encouragement they can get to talk about their reasons.

Something is missing in each of these pictures. Look at the picture and talk about what is missing. The words at the bottom of the page will help you.

A rabbit is supposed to have two _____, but this rabbit has only one.
One _____ is missing.

A spider is supposed to have eight _____, but this spider has only seven.
One _____ is missing.

A fish is supposed to have two _____, but this fish has only one.
One _____ is missing.

A moose is supposed to have two _____, but this moose has only one.
One _____ is missing.

fin   ear   leg   antler

Something is missing in each of these pictures. Look at the picture and talk about what is missing. The words at the bottom of the page will help you.

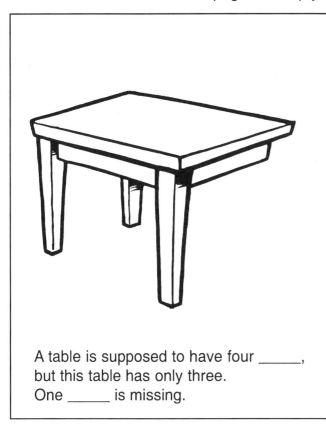

A table is supposed to have four _____, but this table has only three.
One _____ is missing.

A tricycle is supposed to have two _____, but this tricycle has only one.
One _____ is missing.

A bug is supposed to have two _____, but this bug has only one.
One _____ is missing.

A crab is supposed to have two _____, but this crab has only one.
One _____ is missing.

antenna   leg   handlebar   claw

Something is missing in each of these pictures. Look at the picture and talk about what is missing. The words at the bottom of the page will help you.

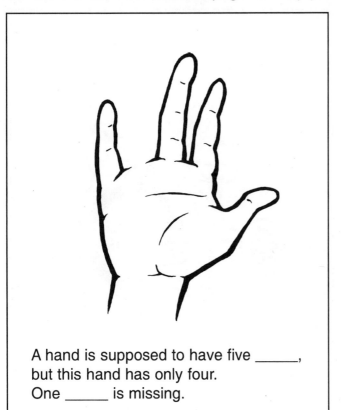

A hand is supposed to have five _____, but this hand has only four.
One _____ is missing.

A cowboy is supposed to have two _____, but this cowboy has only one.
One _____ is missing.

An airplane is supposed to have two _____, but this airplane has only one.
One _____ is missing.

A bicycle is supposed to have two _____, but this bicycle has only one.
One _____ is missing.

boot   wheel   finger   wing

Something is missing in each of these pictures. Look at the picture and talk about what is missing. The words at the bottom of the page will help you.

Sunglasses are supposed to have two _____, but these sunglasses have only one. One _____ is missing.

A child is supposed to have two _____, but this child has only one. One _____ is missing.

A shirt is supposed to have two _____, but this shirt has only one. One _____ is missing.

A rower is supposed to have two _____, but this rower has only one. One _____ is missing.

oar   sleeve   lens   shoe and sock

Something is missing in each of these pictures. Look at the picture and talk about what is missing. The words at the bottom of the page will help you.

A backpack is supposed to have two _____, but this backpack has only one.
One _____ is missing.

This man is supposed to have two _____, but he has only one.
One _____ is missing.

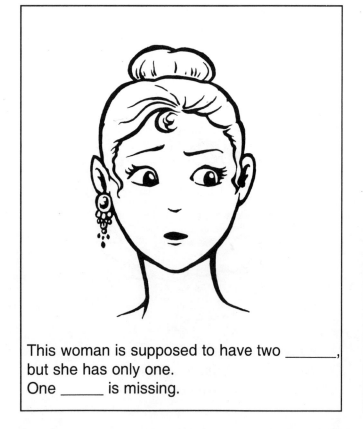

This woman is supposed to have two _____, but she has only one.
One _____ is missing.

A window is supposed to have two _____, but this window has only one.
One _____ is missing.

curtain   suspender   strap   earring

Something is missing in each of these pictures. Look at the picture and talk about what is missing.
The words at the bottom of the page will help you.

A clock is supposed to have two _____,
but this clock has only one.
One _____ is missing.

Scissors are supposed to have two _____,
but these scissors has only one.
One _____ is missing.

A car is supposed to have two _____,
but this car has only one.
One _____ is missing.

A fork is supposed to have four _____,
but this fork has only three.
One _____ is missing.

prong   blade   wiper   hand

Look at the pictures and talk about what is missing. The words at the bottom of the page will help you.

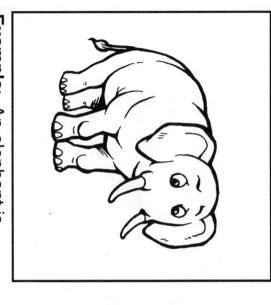

Example: An elephant is supposed to have a trunk. This Elephant's trunk is missing.

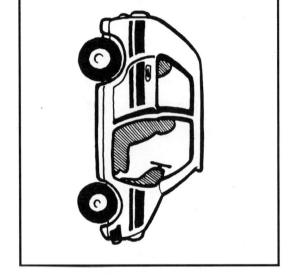

seat   handle   trunk   door   pedal   knob

Introducing Inference

Look at the pictures and talk about what is missing. The words at the bottom of the page will help you.

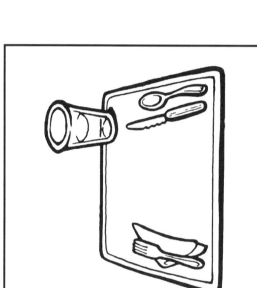

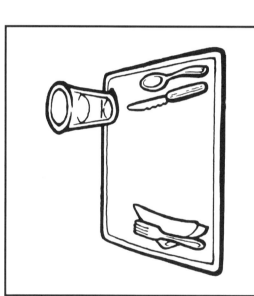

Example: A cup is supposed to have a handle.
This cup's handle is missing.

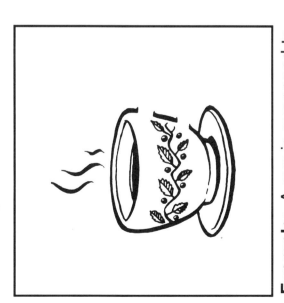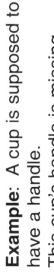

seat handle number step trunk

plate

Look at the pictures and talk about what is missing. The words at the bottom of the page will help you.

Example: An envelope is supposed to have a stamp. This envelope's stamp is missing.

neck   stamp   keys   string   buttons   roof

Introducing Inference

Look at the pictures and talk about what is missing. The words at the bottom of the page will help you.

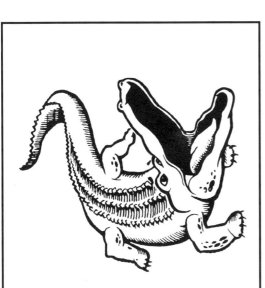

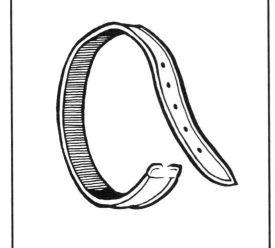

Example: A belt is supposed to have a buckle.
This belt's buckle is missing.

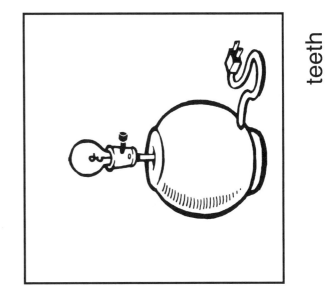

teeth   stem   lid   buckle   shade   mane

Look at the pictures and talk about what is missing. The words at the bottom of the page will help you.

Example: A piano is supposed to have keys. This piano's keys are missing.

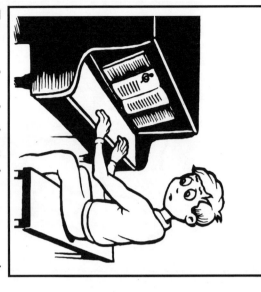

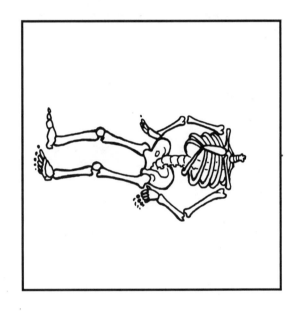

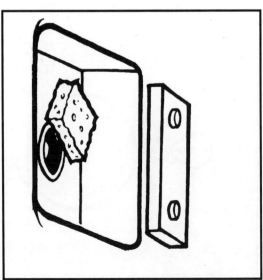

tail   nose   faucet   drawer   head   keys

Look at the pictures and talk about what is missing. The words at the bottom of the page will help you.

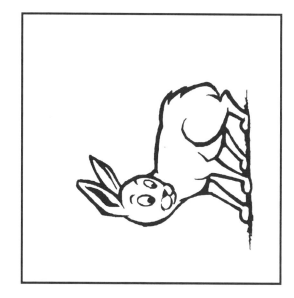

Example: A book is supposed to have pages.
This book's pages are missing.

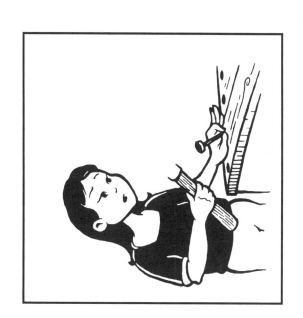

page   burner   handle   blade   tail   head

Here you see a picture sequence, pictures of things or events that are related to each other in time and are shown in order from first to last. The first picture shows what happened first. The second picture shows what happened next. The third picture shows what happened last. Look at this picture sequence. Tell what happened first, next and last.

What happened first?

What happened next?

What happened last?

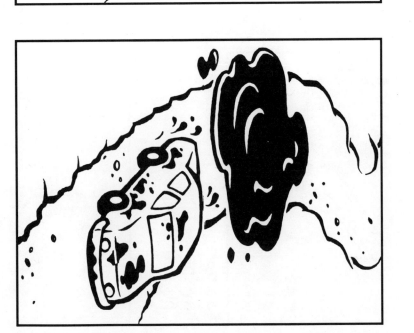

Look at this picture sequence. Tell what happened first, next and last.

What happened last?

What happened next?

What happened first?

Look at this picture sequence. Tell what happened first, next and last.

What happened first?

What happened next?

What happened last?

Introducing Inference

Look at this picture sequence. Tell what happened first, next and last.

What happened last?

What happened next?

What happened first?

Introducing Inference

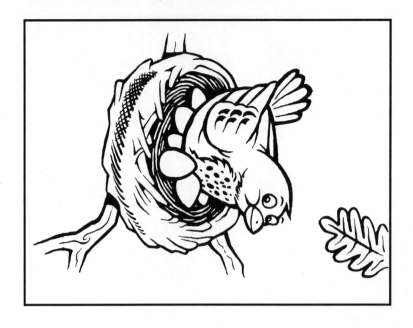

What happened first?

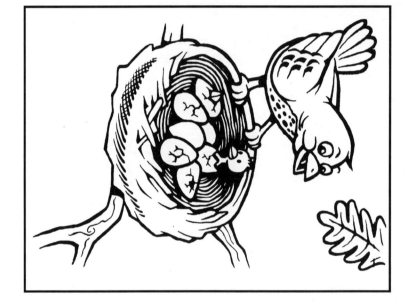

What happened next?

What happened last?

Introducing Inference

Look at this picture sequence. Tell what happened first, next and last.

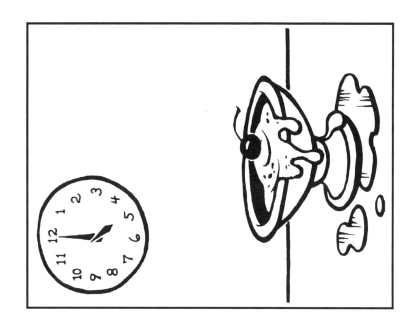

What happened last?

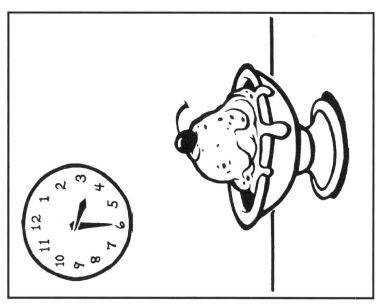

What happened next?

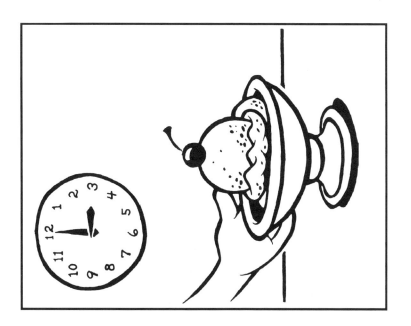

What happened first?

Introducing Inference

Look at this picture sequence. Tell what happened first, next and last.

What happened first?

What happened next?

What happened last?

Introducing Inference

Look at this picture sequence. Tell what happened first, next and last.

What happened last?

What happened next?

What happened first?

Introducing Inference

Look at this picture sequence. Tell what happened first, next and last.

What happened first?

What happened next?

What happened last?

Introducing Inference

Look at this picture sequence. Tell what happened first, next and last.

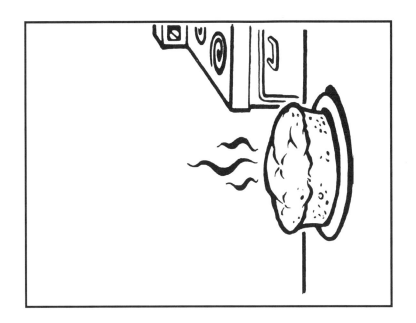

What happened last?

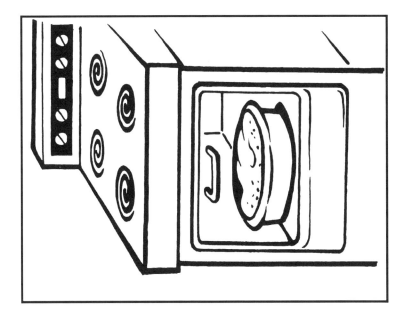

What happened next?

What happened first?

Look at this picture sequence. Tell what happened first, next and last.

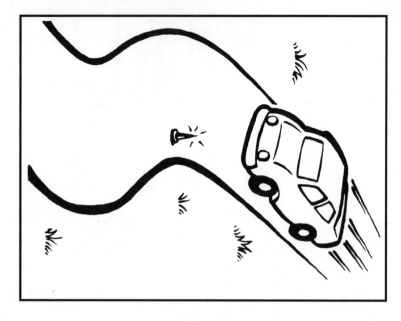

What happened first?

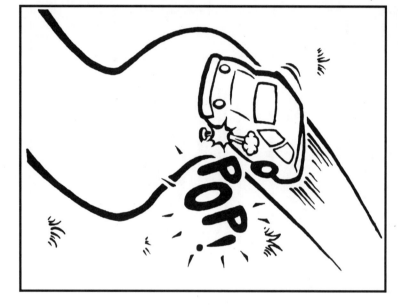

What happened next?

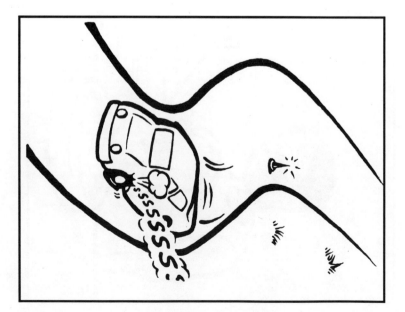

What happened last?

Introducing Inference ©Circuit Publications

Look at this picture sequence. Tell what happened first, next and last.

What happened first?

What happened next?

What happened last?

Introducing Inference

Think about the picture sequences that you saw on pages 14 and 15. Here you see the first and last pictures in those sequences, but the second picture is missing. Try to remember the part that is missing. Then talk about everything that happened in each sequence.

What happened first?

What happened next?

What happened last?

What happened first?

What happened next?

What happened last?

Think about the picture sequences that you saw on pages 16 and 17. Here you see the first and last pictures in those sequences, but the second picture is missing. Try to remember the part that is missing. Then talk about everything that happened in each sequence.

What happened first?

What happened next?

What happened last?

What happened first?

What happened next?

What happened last?

Think about the picture sequences that you saw on pages 18 and 19. Here you see the first and last pictures in those sequences, but the second picture is missing. Try to remember the part that is missing. Then talk about everything that happened in each sequence.

What happened first?

What happened next?

What happened last?

What happened first?

What happened next?

What happened last?

Think about the picture sequences that you saw on pages 20 and 21. Here you see the first and last pictures in those sequences, but the second picture is missing. Try to remember the part that is missing. Then talk about everything that happened in each sequence.

What happened first?

What happened next?

What happened last?

What happened first?

What happened next?

What happened last?

Think about the picture sequences that you saw on pages 22 and 23. Here you see the first and last pictures in those sequences, but the second picture is missing. Try to remember the part that is missing. Then talk about everything that happened in each sequence.

What happened first?

What happened next?

What happened last?

What happened first?

What happened next?

What happened last?

Think about the picture sequences that you saw on pages 24 and 25. Here you see the first and last pictures in those sequences, but the second picture is missing. Try to remember the part that is missing. Then talk about everything that happened in each sequence.

What happened first?

What happened next?

What happened last?

What happened first?

What happened next?

What happened last?

Look at these picture sequences. In each sequence you see the first and second things that happen, but the last box is empty. It is your job to think of what is **probably** going to happen. Tell what you think will probably happen in each of these picture sequences.

What is **probably** going
to happen?

  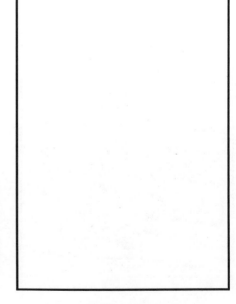

What is **probably** going
to happen?

Introducing Inference

Look at these picture sequences. In each sequence you see the first and second things that happen, but the last box is empty. It is your job to think of what is **probably** going to happen. Tell what you think will probably happen in each of these picture sequences.

What is **probably** going to happen?

What is **probably** going to happen?

Introducing Inference **33**

Look at these picture sequences. In each sequence you see the first and second things that happen, but the last box is empty. It is your job to think of what is **probably** going to happen. Tell what you think will probably happen in each of these picture sequences.

What is **probably** going
to happen?

  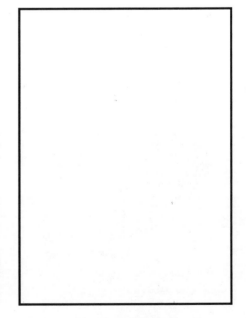

What is **probably** going
to happen?

Look at these picture sequences. In each sequence you see the first and second things that happen, but the last box is empty. It is your job to think of what is **probably** going to happen. Tell what you think will probably happen in each of these picture sequences.

What is **probably** going to happen?

What is **probably** going to happen?

Look at these picture sequences. In each sequence you see the first and second things that happen, but the last box is empty. It is your job to think of what is **probably** going to happen. Tell what you think will probably happen in each of these picture sequences.

What is **probably** going
to happen?

  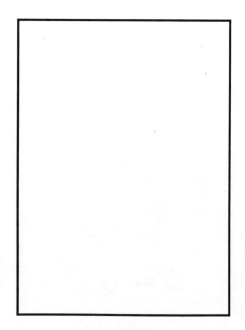

What is **probably** going
to happen?

Introducing Inference

Look at these picture sequences. In each sequence you see the first and second things that happen, but the last box is empty. It is your job to think of what is **probably** going to happen. Tell what you think will probably happen in each of these picture sequences.

What is **probably** going to happen?

What is **probably** going to happen?

Figure out what probably happened in each of these sequences. Look at the first picture, then the last picture in each sequence. Think about what probably happened between the first and last part of each sequence. Find the picture at the bottom of the page that shows what probably happened. Cut and paste the correct picture in the center box of each sequence. Tell why you made your choice.

Introducing Inference

Figure out what probably happened in each of these sequences. Look at the first picture, then the last picture in each sequence. Think about what probably happened between the first and last part of each sequence. Find the picture at the bottom of the page that shows what probably happened. Cut and paste the correct picture in the center box of each sequence. Tell why you made your choice.

Introducing Inference

Figure out what probably happened in each of these sequences. Look at the first picture, then the last picture in each sequence. Think about what probably happened between the first and last part of each sequence. Find the picture at the bottom of the page that shows what probably happened. Cut and paste the correct picture in the center box of each sequence. Tell why you made your choice.

Introducing Inference

Figure out what probably happened in each of these sequences. Look at the first picture, then the last picture in each sequence. Think about what probably happened between the first and last part of each sequence. Find the picture at the bottom of the page that shows what probably happened. Cut and paste the correct picture in the center box of each sequence. Tell why you made your choice.

Figure out what probably happened in each of these sequences. Look at the first picture, then the last picture in each sequence. Think about what probably happened between the first and last part of each sequence. Find the picture at the bottom of the page that shows what probably happened. Cut and paste the correct picture in the center box of each sequence. Tell why you made your choice.

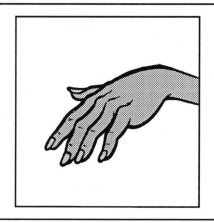

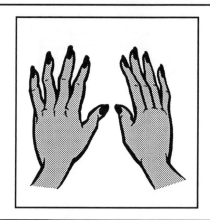

Introducing Inference

Figure out what probably happened in each of these sequences. Look at the first picture, then the last picture in each sequence. Think about what probably happened between the first and last part of each sequence. Find the picture at the bottom of the page that shows what probably happened. Cut and paste the correct picture in the center box of each sequence. Tell why you made your choice.

Tell what probably happened between the first and last parts of each of these sequences. Talk about how you figured out what probably happened.

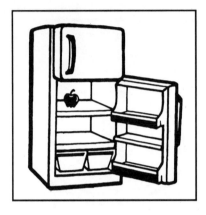  

Introducing Inference

Tell what probably happened between the first and last parts of each of these sequences. Talk about how you figured out what probably happened.

Introducing Inference

Tell what probably happened between the first and last parts of each of these sequences. Talk about how you figured out what probably happened.

Introducing Inference

Tell what probably happened between the first and last parts of each of these sequences. Talk about how you figured out what probably happened.

Look at each of these pictures. Each one shows the last thing that happened in a sequence. Answer the questions and think about what probably happened before.

Look at the peanuts and the peanut shells.

Do you think the peanuts used to be inside their shells?

How do you think the peanuts got out of the shells?

What is stuck all over the boy's face?

Do you think the boy had been chewing the bubble gum?

How did the bubble gum probably get all over the boy's face?

Look at each of these pictures. Each one shows the last thing that happened in a sequence.
Answer the questions and think about what probably happened before.

How does this girl probably feel?

What does the girl see as she looks at her report card?

What do you think the girl did to get grades that made her smile?

What's happening to the building in this picture?

Why do you think the fire truck is near this building?

How do you think the fire fighters probably knew they should come?

Look at each of these pictures. Each one shows the last thing that happened in a sequence. Answer the questions and think about what probably happened before.

What is the dog in this picture doing?

Why did the cat run toward the tree instead of running down the street?

Why do you think the cat is climbing up the tree?

How does the car in this picture look?

Where has this car just been? What happened here?

Why do you think the owner of this car probably took the car to a car wash?

Look at each of these pictures. Each one shows the last thing that happened in a sequence. Answer the questions and think about what probably happened before.

Why do you think one boy is running so fast?

What do you think the other boy is trying to do?

How did the ball get way up in the air? Why is it moving so fast?

What do you see under the Christmas tree?

What do you think is in the stockings hanging on the fireplace?

Who do you think is going up the chimney?

Do you think the presents and treats were there before this person came here?

Look at each of these pictures. Each one shows the last thing that happened in a sequence.
Answer the questions and think about what probably happened before.

What's in this glass?

Where do you think this drink and these ice cubes probably were before?

How do you think the drink and the ice got into the glass?

What do you see in this picture?

How do you think the dog's footprints got onto the floor?

Where could the dog have been before he came inside the house?

Look at each of these pictures. Each one shows the last thing that happened in a sequence. Answer the questions and think about what probably happened before.

Why are the girl and boy so happy? What are they looking at?

Where do you think they probably got all these treats?

Why did they get these treats on this day and not some other day?

What is this man carrying?

What do you think he probably just finished doing?

Why do you think he decided to shovel the snow?

What probably happened the night before or earlier that day?

Look at each of these pictures. Each one shows the last thing that happened in a sequence. Answer the questions and think about what probably happened before.

How do you think this boy feels? Why does he feel this way?

Why is the balloon going up toward the sky?

Where was the balloon before it started to go up?

What should the boy have done so the balloon wouldn't get away?

What is this boy looking at? How do you think he feels?

What probably caused the window to break?

Who do you think did this?

Read each of these sentences and answer the questions asking what happened.

Dad put some food into the dog, Rex's dish when he came home from work. Then he sat down to watch the evening news. When Dad went back into the kitchen he noticed that Rex's dish was empty and Rex was lying on his rug in the corner. What do you think probably happened?

Heather came into the locker room to see if her friend Kelly was there. Heather saw Kelly wearing her swimsuit. She noticed that Kelly's hair was soaking wet. What do you think Kelly had probably been doing before Heather saw her?

When Marcy came home from school she noticed that the mailbox was stuffed full of letters. What had probably happened while Marcy was at school?

Mom gathered up all the wrappings and ribbons and put them into the trash can. While she did this Bobby said good-bye to his friends and started to put his gifts away. What probably happened at Bobby's house before this?

Read each of these sentences and answer the questions asking what happened.

Everyone in the stands stood up and cheered as they watched the football. They cheered louder and louder as the ball got closer to the goal. What do you think probably happened just before this?

Bruce walked his bike up the street and parked it in front of his garage. He went inside the house and told Dad that his bike had a flat tire. Bruce asked if Dad could help put a new tire on the bike. What could have happened to Bruce's bike?

Nancy smelled something burning as she stepped outside. She looked at her neighbor's house across the street and noticed smoke coming out of her neighbor's chimney. What do you think Nancy's neighbors had done before this?

After the storm was over Grandpa walked around the yard outside the house. He noticed that a branch was broken and was about to fall off the tree. This branch was not broken earlier that day. What could have happened to the tree during the storm?

Read each of these sentences and answer the questions asking what happened.

Ted heard the police siren and went over to his window to look outside. He saw a car on the side of the street and a police officer talking to its driver. The officer's car was parked behind this car, and the blue light was still flashing on top of this police car. What do you think probably happened?

Megan ran to the center of the gym and took the trophy from the Mayor. Her volleyball teammates shouted and cheered as they gathered around their coach. The other team walked across the gym and congratulated Megan and her teammates. What had probably happened before this?

Henry looked inside the chicken coop early one morning. There he saw Millie, one of his chickens perched up on a ledge. He looked down and saw two eggs in a bed of straw on the floor below. What do you think happened?

When Donna came home from school Mom told her not to go near the kitchen sink. On the counter Donna saw an empty vase and some fresh cut flowers. What do you think Mom did while Donna was in school that day?

Read each of these sentences and answer the questions asking what happened.

"Mom," said Kenny , "look at this!" Mom turned around and saw Kenny holding his book report up for her to see. She noticed an A+ on the cover of Kenny's report. What do you think happened at school that day?

Mom started to get ready to give Susie a bath. She turned on the water in the bathtub and was ready to call Susie in for her bath. Just then the phone rang. Later Mom came upstairs and saw water running into the tub and over the sides too! What probably happened after the phone rang?

Shelly looked at the bright pink color on her fingernails. She sat still blowing on her nails while they dried. She wanted her nails to look just right for the big dance tonight. What probably happened just before this?

Dad told Pete to hold his hot dog close to the campfire for a little while, just until it was a little dark and plump. Then Dad started to get his own hot dog ready. When he looked at Pete's hot dog he saw that it was all black and withered up. What do you think probably happened to Pete's hot dog?

Read each of these sentences and answer the questions asking what happened.

Mom and Sally packed their dinner in the picnic basket, and got everything ready to go to the beach. Later, when Sally's sister Laura got home she saw the picnic basket and beach toys all ready, but Mom and Sally were still home playing a game. Why do you think Mom and Sally didn't have their picnic on the beach that day?

Mom looked across the table and saw Greg with red sauce on his face and on his shirt. She saw only a few spaghetti noodles left on his plate. Why did Greg probably have red sauce on his face and his shirt?

Dad left the car out in the driveway when he got home from work. Then next day he looked out the window and saw that there was snow all around the car! Dad knew that he'd have to shovel the snow before he could drive to work that day. What probably happened overnight?

Sylvester carried his bag full of food out to his car. He was thinking about the delicious dinner that he planned to prepare later. What had Sylvester been doing before this?

Read each of these sentences and answer the questions asking what happened.

Whitney told her friend Mike that it was okay to work on his project and use her tools inside her garage. She came home from work expecting to find Mike working on his project. Instead, she found all the tools where they belong, and a pile of saw dust swept neatly over in the corner. What did Mike probably do?

Jane parked her car outside the building and hurried in for her appointment. When she came out she noticed a parking ticket on her window. What had probably happened while Jane was inside the building?

Nancy removed her groceries from the bag when she got home from the store. The first thing she found, right on top, was a watermelon. Next she found lettuce, apples and cheese. On the bottom of the bag she found potato chips and eggs. The chips were crushed into small pieces, and the eggs were broken. What probably happened?

Jenny waved to her neighbor Hank as he drove home from work. She noticed that Hank's truck was all muddy. She knew that his truck was all shiny and clean that morning. What probably happened to Hank's truck that day?

In the second part of this book students will use their inference skills to solve simple problems. it is important to remind students that this means they draw inference by following three steps:

1. Think about the information that is given and determine what information is missing.

2. Identify and supply the missing information using their knowledge and background experience.

3. Combine the information given and the information supplied.

Students working through these activities should always be asked to tell how they solved the problem. They should tell how they identified the missing information and how they filled this in.

Aside from following these guidelines in solving inference problems students gain experience in thinking in terms of probability. Notice words, phrases and sentences such as *probably*, *might have*, *could have* and *What do you think?* occurring frequently in these pages. It is most important that students understand that when they use inference in solving problems they are using their best judgement.

The tasks in Part Two deal with particular types of inferences and/or types of missing information. Following is a brief discussion of the kinds of problems you will find here.

Pages 62–67 present items where students are asked, "What **probably happened**?" This is similar to activities on pages 26–31 and 38–43 in Part One of this book. Students are given an outcome and asked what probably lead to this outcome.

Pages 68–73 present items asking "What is someone **ready to do**?" In each item on these pages someone is preparing to do something. Hints as to what they are getting ready to do are given within these statements.

Pages 74–80 present items asking **Who?** In each statement a quote from someone is given, and students must judge who would likely have said this. Suggested answers for items on these pages are found on page 81. These can be shown to students as they work through the tasks on a page or not. Younger students might need these references, older students might benefit from the challenge of recalling the answers without being given clues. For our language students, focusing on the vocabulary in these pages along with the problem-solving task, can be a benefit.

Pages 82–87 present items asking **What?** In each statement a particular thing is referred to, hints are included in the statement, then students must figure out what. Suggested answers for each of these questions can be found on page 88. Students are encouraged to use their best judgement in answering these questions. These questions could be answered correctly in more than one way. The answers presented represent only one possibility.

Pages 89–96 present items asking **Where?** Here students are given a description of a situation and asked where this event is taking place. Answers for the items on these eight pages are available on page 97.

Pages 98–100 present items asking **When?** Here students are given situations and asked questions involving time factors.

Pages 101–112 focus on the notion that more than one event might cause something to happen. Here students are given a situation and asked what probably happened. They are given three choices, any of which are likely except one. The task is to identify which one of the choices could not have likely caused this outcome.

Read about each of these situations and tell what might have happened. Tell **why** you think this is so. Remember some information is missing here, and it is up to you to figure out what happened.

1. Dad tiptoed out of the baby's room and motioned for all of us to be quiet. What do you think probably happened just before this?

2. Marian was driving down the road when she saw a sign ahead saying that the road was closed. She saw some cars stopped up ahead, and some cars or trucks with red lights flashing. What do you think happened just before?

3. Barry walked toward his car parked on the street. He noticed that one side of the back of the car was lower than the front of the car. What happened?

4. Everyone was surprised to see Henry come to school on crutches Monday morning. What could have happened to Henry over the weekend?

5. When Larry came home from school he could smell something delicious and chocolate all through the house. What could have happened while Larry was at school?

6. Melanie opened the squeaky back door when she went to work in the morning. When she came home the door didn't squeak when she opened it. What could have happened while Melanie was at work?

7. Penny's friends were surprised when she came into school this morning. She didn't have her long braids! Instead, Penny had short curly hair. What probably happened yesterday?

8. Harvey smelled smoke when he stepped outside his house this evening. What could have happened somewhere in Harvey's neighborhood?

9. When Greg came home he found no mail in his mailbox, but found a note from the mailman on the front door next to the mailbox. What probably happened earlier that day?

10. The Jacksons came home from their ski trip last winter and their house was freezing cold. What could have happened while they were away?

11. Mr. Russo thought his number was picked in last night's lottery, but he couldn't prove it. What probably happened? How do you know?

Read about each of these situations and tell what might have happened. Tell **why** you think this is so. Remember some information is missing here, and it is up to you to figure out what happened.

1. As Nancy walked home after school she saw her grandma's car in the driveway. What probably happened earlier that day? How do you know?

2. Dave walked into the kitchen and saw a pot boiling over on the stove. What could have happened before Dave walked into the kitchen? How do you know?

3. Mom washed the dirt and blood from Willie's scraped knee and put a bandage over the sore. What do you think had just happened to Willie? How do you know?

4. Sharon took her presents up to her room and put them away. Then she started to write thank-you notes to her friends. What probably happened before she did this? How do you know?

5. When Mr. Morgan got home he saw water on the window sill and on the floor under the window. What probably happened while Mr. Morgan was away? How do you know?

6. Sue walked toward the stove when she heard the timer go off. What probably happened before this? How do you know ?

7. When the Kennedys came home Tommy saw that there were two messages on their answering machine. What probably happened at the Kennedy's house while they were away? How do you know?

8. Katie went over to look out her window when she heard the siren. What might have happened? How do you know?

9. Scottie knocked the snow off his boots and brushed snow off his jacket. then he went inside the house and took off his mittens, hat, jacket and his boots. What probably happened before this? How do you know?

10. Angie heard her dog Pepper outside at the back door. When she saw Pepper she was surprised to see mud all over his feet and his legs. What do you think Pepper did before he came home? How do you know?

11. Jessica tried to take a shower this morning, but only cold water came out of the shower head. What probably happened? How do you know?

Read about each of these situations and tell what might have happened. Tell **why** you think this is so. Remember some information is missing here, and it is up to you to figure out what happened.

1. Molly is a very good player on her soccer team. Early in the season Molly hurt her ankle and had a cast on it for three weeks. Molly's team ended up in last place in their city league. What probably happened to cause the team to lose so many games? How do you know?

2. Jimmy looked at his plate and watched the butter melt on his corn on the cob. The corn was too hot to pick up. What probably happened to the corn before this? How do you know?

3. Dad and the children unbuckled their seat belts and got out of the car. What had Dad and the children just done? How do you know?

4. Margie took the basket of clean laundry upstairs, folded the clothes and towels and put them away. What do you think Margie did before this? How do you know?

5. Mom heard the car horn beep. She picked up her bag, went out the front door and got into the car. Why do you think Mom did this? How do you know?

6. Judy saw her brother coming from the orchard with a basket of fresh apples. What do you think happened? How do you know?

7. Kenny put his new jeans on and went out to play. When he came in there was a hole in his jeans near his right knee. What probably happened? How do you know?

8. Bonnie got a new dress last summer to wear for her sister's wedding this year. A week before the wedding Bonnie tried the dress on, and it was too small for her. What do you think happened? How do you know?

9. Perky, the kitten, ate some of the food from her dish while Barkley, the dog, was asleep. When Perky came back later to finish her food the dish was empty. What probably happened? How do you know?

10. Ben sat quietly on the dock holding his fishing rod out into the lake. Suddenly he felt something pulling at his fishing line. What probably happened? How do you know?

Read about each of these situations and tell what might have happened. Tell **why** you think this is so. Remember some information is missing here, and it is up to you to figure out what happened.

1. Jack and Ronnie stood inside while Dad waited in line to buy tickets for the movie. Dad walked into the lobby looking disappointed. What do you think happened? How do you know?

2. When Grandma went out to pick the lettuce from her garden there were holes in many of the lettuce leaves. What could have happened? How do you know?

3. This morning on the way to the State Park everyone looked at the cows and horses grazing on grass in fields along the road. On the way home they couldn't see the cows or horses. They couldn't even see the fields! What probably happened? How do you know?

4. When Mr. Michaels came home from work he saw the mixer and some ingredients for cookies out on the counter, but no one was home. What might have happened? How do you know?

5. The burglar sneaked up to the side window of the house. When he started to open the window something surprised him and he ran away. What could have happened? How do you know?

6. The batter started to run around the bases after she hit the ball, but she never ran to home plate and scored a run. What could have happened? How do you know?

7. The birds sat peacefully on the backyard fence. Suddenly they all began to fly away. What could have happened? How do you know?

8. Jan saw a large wet spot on the ceiling in the corner of the kitchen. She also saw water on the wall under the wet spot. What could have happened?

9. As Danny walked to school he noticed that his backpack felt lighter than usual. What could have happened? How do you know?

10. Mia thought that everyone had forgotten that today was her birthday. When she got home she knew she was wrong. What could have happened? How do you know?

Read about each of these situations and tell what might have happened. Tell **why** you think this is so. Remember some information is missing here, and it is up to you to figure out what happened.

1. When Mr. Stenson came home from work he was surprised to see pieces of broken glass and a baseball on his living room floor. The living room window was broken. What do you think happened? How do you know?

2. When Donnie tried to rent a video from the video store he was told that he had to pay a penalty fee before he could rent another video. What probably happened? How do you know?

3. Mr. Fowler had to call a plumber because the water would not go down the drain in the kitchen sink. What could have happened? How do you know?

4. When Maggie got home from the dance she carefully took some loose pearls and a broken string out of her bag. What probably happened? How do you know?

5. As Jamie walked down the street he saw a furnace service truck parked in front of his house. What probably happened? How do you know?

6. Carrie's favorite TV show is on every Tuesday at eight o'clock on Channel 4. Last Tuesday when Carrie turned on Channel 4 Carrie's favorite show wasn't on. What could have happened? How do you know?

7. Yesterday morning when the Smiths woke up their lights, radio, TV, electric stove and toaster were not working. What could have happened? How do you know?

8. Wally had to call his mom and tell her that he was being punished and had to stay after school. What do you think happened? How do you know?

9. Last Sunday morning Bobby tried to find the Comics Section in the newspaper, but this section was missing. What could have happened to the comics? How do you know?

10. When the Ryans came home from the restaurant they saw that the door of their pet hamster's cage was opened and their little hamster was not in his cage. What could have happened? How do you know?

Read about each of these situations and tell what might have happened. Tell **why** you think this is so. Remember some information is missing here, and it is up to you to figure out what happened.

1. Jerry stepped up to the counter and ordered an ice cream sundae. When he looked down he saw some money on the floor. How could that money have gotten there? How do you know?

2. Karen couldn't fall asleep because their neighbor's dog Fred was barking. She thought this was strange because Fred usually stays outside and doesn't bark at night. What could have happened that caused Fred to bark? How do you know?

3. Robin took her books out of her book bag and put them in her desk when she got to school. The book report that she did the night before wasn't with her books. She was upset because it was due that day. What probably happened to Robin's book report? How do you know?

4. Cindy got off the plane and went down to pick up her suitcase at the baggage claim section in the airport. She picked up her bag from the carousel and quickly went out to her car. When she got home and opened her bag her things were not inside. Rather, someone else's clothes and shoes were inside! What probably happened? How do you know?

5. Monte filled the bird feeder that hangs from a tree near his window. He did this late at night so he'd enjoy watching birds outside his window the next day. When Monte looked out early the next morning the feeder was empty. He knew the birds couldn't have eaten all that food overnight. What could have happened to all that food? How do you know?

6. Jenny and her mom made a snowman last Saturday using the fresh snow that had fallen overnight. Before Jenny went to sleep that night she called her friend Liz to come and see her snowman the next day. Jenny stayed inside all day waiting for Liz to come. When Liz arrived, the girls went outside to look at the snowman. They were surprised to see no snowman, only wet, muddy grass! What could have happened to the snowman? How do you know?

7. Gabby happily took the balloon from the clown. As she walked down the street she held the balloon's string first in one hand, then the other. Then she felt the balloon string moving up out of her hand, but nobody was pulling the string out of her hand. What could have happened to the balloon? How do you know?

8. Jasmine cleared a place on her bathroom counter. She laid out her liquid make-up, her blush, her lipstick and her eye shadow. She pulled her hair back and washed her face. What was Jasmine ready to do? How do you know?

Think about what must be done before you can do something. You have to get ready! Read about these people and think about what they are **getting ready to do**. Then talk about the clues that gave you your ideas.

1. Sol put some bread, a knife and a plate on the table. Then he got some peanut butter and jelly from the refrigerator. What is Sol ready to do? How do you know?

2. Maureen loves to baby-sit for her neighbor and take care of her little girl, Angie. After Maureen gives Angie her dinner and plays with her for a while she helps Angie put her toys away. Then she gives Angie a bath and helps her put her pajamas on. Finally, Maureen reads Angie a story. What is Angie ready to do? How do you know?

3. Paul drove his car over to the side of the road. He got his tools and his spare tire out of the trunk. He picked up his jack. What was Paul ready to do? How do you know?

4. Craig moved all the papers from the computer table. He set his note cards and outlines down on the table and turned on the computer. Then he opened a new file. What was Craig ready to do? How do you know?

5. Ellen found her recipe. She went to the store and bought a crust and some sauce. She bought some shredded cheese to sprinkle on top. She came home and cut some onions, peppers and sliced some pepperoni. She got a large flat round pan from the cupboard. What was she ready to do? How do you know?

6. Roy thought about his girlfriend's birthday and wanted it to be special. He knew when he'd like to help celebrate her birthday, and made a list of friends to call. What was Roy ready to do? How do you know?

7. Mom and Jeff went to the farm to choose a pumpkin. When they got home they spread newspaper out on the kitchen table. They got a sharp knife, a black marker and a bowl for the seeds. What were Mom and Jeff ready to do? How do you know?

8. Dad decided that most of the leaves had fallen from the trees in the front yard. Then he bought some large plastic bags and got the rake from the garage. What was Dad ready to do? How do you know?

9. Margaret got her shampoo from the closet. She got a towel ready, and set her hair dryer and her brush out on the counter. What was Margaret ready to do? How do you know?

Think about what must be done before you can do something. You have to get ready! Read about these people and think about what they are **getting ready to do**. Then talk about the clues that gave you your ideas.

1. Theo made his airline and hotel reservations over a month ago. Last week he bought a new swim suit, sun glasses and some tennis balls. Earlier today he packed his suitcase and asked his friend to take care of his dog next week. In the morning Theo will call a cab to take him to the airport. What's Theo getting ready to do? How do you know?

2. Max put his boots and warm hat on. He put on his coat and mittens and walked out to the garage to get his sled. What is Max getting ready to do? How do you know?

3. Dad and Ryan gathered some wood and cleared a spot near the picnic bench. They arranged the wood so they could build a nice fire. Mom and Brad got hamburgers ready and got the drinks, rolls, mustard, catsup and pickles from the cooler and the plates and napkins from inside their tent. What was the family getting ready to do? How do you know?

4. Aunt Mary measured her windows then went to the store to choose some fabric. She cut the pieces of fabric a little longer than the size of the windows, then threaded the needle in her sewing machine. What was Aunt Mary ready to do? How do you know?

5. Jane pulled into the gas station and drove her car up to the gas pump. She lifted the hose and nozzle from the pump and removed the cap from her gas tank. What was Jane ready to do? How do you know?

6. Joey put a bowl, a spoon and an ice cream scoop on the table. He got the chocolate syrup and nuts from the cupboard, whipped cream from the refrigerator and ice cream from the freezer. What was Joey ready to do? How do you know?

7. Dave took all the food from his refrigerator. He decided which things he could save and use later and which could not be eaten and should be thrown away. He got a bowl of warm soapy water and a cloth. What was Dave ready to do? How do you know?

8. Melinda found a box, some wrapping paper, scissors, tape and ribbon. She put the necklace that she bought for her friend into a small box. What was Melinda ready to do? How do you know?

9. George moved the furniture from the dining room. He took the curtains off the window. Then he got his ladder and cleaned the walls. He found his paintbrushes and rollers. He went to the hardware store to buy the other things he needed. What was George almost ready to do? How do you know?

Think about what must be done before you can do something. You have to get ready! Read about these people and think about what they are **getting ready to do**. Then talk about the clues that gave you your ideas.

1. Colleen looked at all her winter skirts and pants and thought of a color that would go with many of her outfits. She went to the yarn store and bought some knitting needles and yarn and some buttons. Then she measured her chest and her arms. What was Colleen ready to do? How do you know?

2. Ned put a large metal tub outside and filled it with water. He got the special bottle of pet shampoo and a large brush. Then he called his dog, Rufus. What was Ned ready to do? How do you know?

3. Mom got some film at the store and put it into her camera. She told Molly and Bret just where to stand, then stepped back a few steps. She told the children to smile. What was Mom ready to do? How do you know?

4. Dan drove his car up the driveway. He closed all the windows, then got a bucket, some soap and window cleaner, a soft cloth and a towel. What was Dan ready to do? How do you know?

5. Nelson sliced some cheese, got some bread and some butter. He got a knife and a spatula, put a large frying pan on the stove and turned on the burner. What was Nelson ready to do? How do you know?

6. The doctor told Chad to sit back in the chair. Then he turned on a special light and got a flat piece of wood from the jar on his counter. He told Chad to put his head back and open his mouth wide. What was the doctor ready to do? How do you know?

7. Laura got into the plane and sat down in front of the controls. She fastened her seat belt, listened for instructions from the control tower, and taxied toward the runway. What was Laura ready to do? How do you know?

8. Sharon found some old baggy pants and her dad's old shirt and old hat. She got some make up and a mask that covered the top of her face. What do you think Sharon was ready to do? How do you know?

9. Tyler brought the bundle of this morning's newspapers into the house. He folded each one and put it into a plastic bag. Then he put the newspapers into his sack. He got his jacket and hat on and put the sack of newspapers over his shoulder. What was Tyler ready to do? How do you know?

Think about what must be done before you can do something. You have to get ready! Read about these people and think about what they are **getting ready to do**. Then talk about the clues that gave you your ideas.

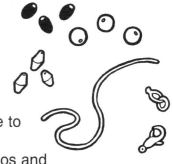

1. Paula poured her beautiful beads onto the table. She got some special string to string the beads and a clasp to put at the ends of the string. What was Paula ready to do? How do you know?

2. Carlos and his friend Tommy walked along the trail until they came to a little stream of cool clear water. Then they took their socks and shoes off and rolled their pants up to their knees. What were Carlos and Tommy ready to do? How do you know?

3. Dad took his pad and sketching pens and climbed to the top of the hill. He looked around then sat down facing the most beautiful view. He took out his pens and paper. What was Dad about to do? How do you know?

4. Mom gave little Jackie a bath and washed his hair. She dried him off, put his robe on and got his comb and brush and her scissors. She combed Jackie's hair straight down and picked up her scissors. What was Mom ready to do? How do you know?

5. Dad got his tools from the basement and set them out on the kitchen floor. He shut off the water all over the house. Then he set up a light under the sink and got his wrench. What do you think Dad was ready to do? How do you know?

6. Roy put on his mask and chest protector and stooped down behind home plate. He put on his mitt and waited for the batter to step up to the plate. Then he looked straight at the pitcher. What was Roy ready to do? How do you know?

7. Sonny put the blender on the counter and got a tall glass from the cupboard. He got some ice cream, chocolate syrup, milk and an ice cream scoop and put them on the counter. What was Sonny ready to do? How do you know?

8. Mark filled his water bottle and put on his helmet. He went out to the garage and put a little more air in both tires. What was Mark ready to do? How do you know?

9. Rich looked around his room. Then he got the vacuum cleaner, some dust cloths and some spray cleaner and came back to his room. What was Rich ready to do? How do you know?

Think about what must be done before you can do something. You have to get ready! Read about these people and think about what they are **getting ready to do**. Then talk about the clues that gave you your ideas.

1. Cindy peeled some fresh apples and sliced them. She mixed some flower, water, salt and butter until it was mixed together in a soft ball. Then she rolled out the dough and put it in the pan for the crust. She got some sugar and cinnamon out of the cupboard and turned the oven on. What was Cindy ready to do? How do you know?

2. Mike thought that his flower garden looked messy. He went into the garage and got a long handled garden tool, a pad to kneel on and a big plastic bag. Then he went back to the flower garden, put gardening gloves on and knelt down. What was Mike ready to do? How do you know?

3. Marshall walked to the end of the board. He looked down into the water, raised his arms straight above his head with fingertips touching. What was Marshall ready to do? How do you know?

4. Vince stood among the others in the excited crowd. He really wanted the beautiful painting up on the stage. Someone in the crowd raised her arm and shouted "Two hundred dollars!" Someone else shouted "Two fifty!" Vince looked in his wallet and raised his arm. What was Vince ready to do? How do you know?

5. Margaret walked slowly up the aisle holding her bouquet. Everyone in the church was standing, looking at her. She looked straight ahead at her fiancé standing at the front of the church next to the minister. What was Margaret ready to do? How do you know?

6. Jim picked up the heavy black ball and put his two middle fingers and thumb into the holes. He looked straight down the alley and saw all ten pins standing up in place. He swung the heavy ball back and started to take big running steps. What was Jim ready to do? How do you know?

7. Fred walked up to the table and signed the back of his paycheck. He filled out a slip of paper and stood in line behind three other people. He thought he'd probably save some of the money from this week's pay and use the rest to buy things he needed. What was Fred ready to do? How do you know?

8. Paul climbed up all the steps in the bell tower of the church. When he was on the highest step he grabbed the heavy rope that hung from the bell. What was Paul ready to do? How do you know?

Think about what must be done before you can do something. You have to get ready! Read about these people and think about what they are **getting ready to do**. Then talk about the clues that gave you your ideas.

1. Gina bought a large bag of fresh lemons and brought them home. She made sure there were plenty of ice cubes in the freezer. She squeezed juice from the lemons, poured it into a pitcher and put in some sugar. What was she ready to do? How do you know?

2. Dad carefully took the parts of Timmy's new wagon out of the box and looked at the picture of the wagon on the front of the box. He got his tools and read the instructions that came with the wagon. What was Dad ready to do? How do you know?

3. Steve took his customer's order. Then he went back and sliced a banana lengthwise down the center and laid the banana in a long deep bowl. He got his ice cream scoop and opened the freezer and put one scoop each of vanilla, chocolate and strawberry ice cream on top of the banana. Then he put some chocolate and strawberry toppings on the ice cream and squirted whipped cream over the whole thing. What was Steve's customer ready to do? How do you know?

4. Millie got dressed and put on her helmet. She went out to the stable and put Prince's saddle and bridal on him. She took the reins and led him from his stall out onto the path. What was Millie ready to do? How do you know?

5. Paula sorted her dirty clothes, putting light colors and dark colors into separate baskets. She got the box of soap from the cupboard. What was Paula ready to do? How do you know?

6. Bret went into the food storage center at the zoo. He took several large slabs of meat from the refrigerator and a bag of dry food from the shelf. Then he headed out to the lions' and tigers' areas. What was Bret ready to do? How do you know?

7. Bob is going to the new products division of a car maker next week. He has his drawings and all the research data and a video showing how his new invention will allow cars of the future to go 300 miles on one gallon of gasoline! What was Bob ready to do? How do you know?

8. Maria scrubbed herself clean and sterile. Her assistant helped her put on her sterile clothes. She put on her gloves and checked her instruments. A bright light shined down on her patient as he lay in a deep sleep on the table. She asked the nurse to hand her a scalpel. What was Maria ready to do? How do you know?

Read each of the items below. Think about **who** probably said them. For each item tell how you figured this out.

1. "Will everyone please be seated and move to the back of the bus!" Who probably said this? How do you know?

2. "Take out your math workbooks and open them to page 72." Who probably said this? How do you know?

3. "Our specials this evening are chicken parmigiana and a summer fruit sampler." Who probably said this? How do you know?

4. "I won't put fertilizer around these bushes until next month." Who probably said this? How do you know?

5. "Do you want to deposit this money in your checking or your savings account?" Who probably said this? How do you know?

6. "We've been cleared for landing. We should be in Chicago in twenty minutes." Who probably said this? How do you know?

7. "I'm going to give your dog her rabies vaccination after her check-up today." Who probably said this? How do you know?

8. "How short do you want your hair cut today?" Who probably said this? How do you know?

9. "Last week I played the role of Queen Elizabeth." Who probably said this? How do you know?

10. "We're trying to rescue the people inside, but the smoke is very heavy." Who probably said this? How do you know?

11. "Looks like we'll have the walls done by the end of the week. We'll start the roof on Monday." Who probably said this? How do you know?

12. "My specialties are French meat dishes, but I have some experience preparing Italian foods." Who probably said this? How do you know?

13. "Just keep your eye on the ball. Don't pay attention to that runner on second base." Who probably said this? How do you know?

Introducing Inference

Read each of the items below. Think about **who** probably said them. For each item tell how you figured this out.

1. "'Hope we have good weather this week. We've got to get that corn crop in." Who probably said this? How do you know?

2. "I think you'll need to rewire this whole house. Some of this old wiring could cause a fire." Who probably said this? How do you know?

3. "My latest book is a mystery story. It'll be published this fall." Who probably said this? How do you know?

4. "Ladies and Gentlemen of the jury, have you reached a verdict?" Who probably said this? How do you know?

5. "Teachers, please remind your students to give their parents the information about our holiday program." Who probably said this? How do you know?

6. "Last season I ran a thousand yards and caught over a hundred passes." Who probably said this? How do you know?

7. "What kind of cake would you like, white or chocolate? Also please choose butter cream or chocolate frosting." Who probably said this? How do you know?

8. "I'm afraid we couldn't get this spot off your jacket." Who probably said this? How do you know?

9. "We had a great day at sea! Must have brought in 200 lobsters." Who probably said this? How do you know?

10. "You'll find that book in the Geography Section. The books are arranged on the shelves in alphabetical order by the author's last name." Who probably said this? How do you know?

11. "We apologize for this interruption. We're having some technical difficulties in our broadcasting studio." Who probably said this? How do you know?

12. "Looks like you're in excellent health today. Come back for a check-up in a year." Who probably said this? How do you know?

Read each of the items below. Think about **who** probably said them. For each item tell how you figured this out.

1. "The bride and groom should come up and say their vows when the music stops. I'll perform the ceremony and give a little talk, then the bride and groom will lead the procession down the aisle." Who probably said this? How do you know?

2. "If I'm elected I promise to introduce a bill to lower our taxes. I appreciate your vote!" Who probably said this? How do you know?

3. "It'll probably need two coats. This dark color will probably show through with just one coat." Who probably said this? How do you know?

4. "Our pork chops and rib roasts are prime quality, and we make the best sausage in town." Who probably said this? How do you know?

5. "I'll be down in the furnace room working on installing a new thermostat. I'll plan to fix the door hinges in Ms. Casey's third grade classroom first thing tomorrow." Who probably said this? How do you know?

6. "Both of you should enter from left. Move quickly and look at the person behind the desk. You're supposed to look nervous and upset. The camera will zoom in on your faces as you move toward the desk." Who probably said this? How do you know?

7. "I can use oak or maple wood to make this table. Both are very strong and can be smoothed out very nicely." Who probably said this? How do you know?

8. "I'm going to have to drive all the way around the square because 68th Street is closed, but I'll get you to the court house as fast as I can." Who probably said this? How do you know?

9. "One of the new features in this model is side airbags. Air conditioning, automatic transmission and leather seats are standard. Gets better mileage than last year's model." Who probably said this? How do you know?

10. "Do you want this to go regular parcel post or priority mail? Priority mail is faster." Who probably said this? How do you know?

11. "All hands on deck! There's a storm coming, and we've got to get ready!" Who probably said this? How do you know?

Introducing Inference

Read each of the items below. Think about **who** probably said them. For each item tell how you figured this out.

1. "Lead with your right foot and take two steps to the right. Then take two steps to the left. Twirl your partner around. Then take two steps together." Who probably said this? How do you know?

2. "We'd better contact mission control. We might have to delay hooking up with the space station". Who probably said this? How do you know?

3. "I can make this puppet sound like a little boy and that one sound like an older man." Who probably said this? How do you know?

4. "If the clay is just right I can form the base and begin to shape the body quickly, then work on the details later." Who probably said this? How do you know?

5. "I'll give you credit for your call. Would you like me to try that number for you?" Who probably said this? How do you know?

6. "We'll be able to put the shingles over most of the area today. We'll have do some repair work around the chimney before we can put shingles down in that area." Who probably said this? How do you know?

7. "You should do some stretching exercises before you do your aerobics, then stretch your muscles again at the end of your workout." Who probably said this? How do you know?

8. "Timber!" Who probably said this? How do you know?

9. "This refrigerator needs a new temperature monitor control. It's not keeping food cold because this part is not working." Who probably said this? How do you know?

10. . . . "And now I'll do a number from my new CD. It was written by a good friend who also accompanied me on the guitar during the recording." Who probably said this? How do you know?

11. "Temperatures should be in the mid-thirties overnight, and possibly get as high as 50 tomorrow. We'll be watching that cold front that's moving in, looking for possible snow for the weekend." Who probably said this? How do you know?

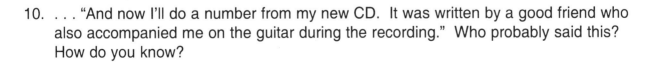

Read each of the items below. Think about **who** probably said them. For each item tell how you figured this out.

1. "You were going 55 in a 45 mile an hour zone. May I see your license?" Who probably said this? How do you know?

2. "Everyone out of the water! Go into the club house until the storm passes, then everyone can go back in." Who probably said this? How do you know?

3. "If this feels comfortable I'll adjust the lenses for you and you could wear them home." Who probably said this? How do you know?

4. "We can design this site so that your customers can order products from your company using the internet." Who probably said this? How do you know?

5. "Falling from 3,000 feet over this beautiful meadow is just a beautiful experience. I just hope my parachute opens!" Who probably said this? How do you know?

6. "The string section should start off soft, then build to a nice loud tone, then the percussion section will come in dramatically, then fade as the French horn solo begins." Who probably said this? How do you know?

7. "I want to get to the shore early so I can capture the sunrise in my painting." Who probably said this? How do you know?

8. "I'll have to shut the water off all over the house while I replace these pipes under your kitchen sink." Who probably said this? How do you know?

9. "We'll stay on this track until we're near the city. Then we'll have to switch tracks. Then we'll have to change from the diesel over to the electric locomotive." Who probably said this? How do you know?

10. "Please remove your groceries from your cart and put them on the check-out counter. I'll scan each item to get the price. We take cash, checks or credit cards." Who probably said this? How do you know?

11. "We're going to enter the room where the paintings from the Eighteenth Century are displayed. I'll tell you something about each of the artists as we view their work." Who probably said this? How do you know?

Introducing Inference

Read each of the items below. Think about **who** probably said them. For each item tell how you figured this out.

1. "When I walked down the runway the spotlight shined on me. I listened to the announcer tell the audience about the beautiful clothes I was wearing and turned so that the audience could see the front and back of my outfit." Who probably said this? How do you know?

2. "Every night I do silly tricks for the audience while the animal or high wire acts set up to perform. I love to hear everyone laughing at my tricks." Who probably said this? How do you know?

3. "This is a big story. I'll stay here at the scene until I have to leave to write my piece and get it in on time to go to press." Who probably said this? How do you know?

4. "My dear fellow countrymen and women, my wife, the queen, and I wish to express our joy and our thanks to all of you on this great day." Who probably said this? How do you know?

5. "Looks like your take-off will have to be delayed until we can check out the strange noise in this jet engine." Who probably said this? How do you know?

6. "After you complete the experiment, write a report on your findings in your lab notebooks." Who probably said this? How do you know?

7. "Pick a card, any card. Now put it back in the stack. I'll cover the cards and say the magic words. When we uncover the stack, your card will be on top." Who probably said this? How do you know?

8. "If you need to make a call do it now, because your service will be cut off all morning. I have to install this new communication switching system." Who probably said this? How do you know?

9. "Your teeth look pretty good this time, but you should floss them more often. The dentist will be in to check your teeth in a minute." Who probably said this? How do you know?

10. "Take your ticket stub with you and leave your keys in the car. When you return, we'll bring your car to you here in front of this building." Who probably said this? How do you know?

Read each of the items below. Think about **who** probably said them. For each item tell how you figured this out.

1. "I'm going to take your temperature and blood pressure now and mark your chart." Who probably said this? How do you know?

2. "I'll be using silks and velvets for my evening gowns. I'll use bright colored cottons and linens for my daytime dresses." Who probably said this? How do you know?

3. "I think this skirt should be hemmed just a little shorter." Who probably said this? How do you know?"

4. "The troops in our platoon have completed their mission, Sir." Who probably said this? How do you know?

5. "These plants do best in the shade. Those need a lot of sun." Who probably said this? How do you know?

6. "I think these are too big for you. Your foot is slipping out at the heel when you walk. I'll see if we have this style in a smaller size." Who probably said this? How do you know?

7. "I worked really hard to play this waltz. It was hard at first, but now when I start to play I feel like my fingers are dancing over the keys!" Who probably said this? How do you know?

8. "Let's try a little blue eye shadow to make your eyes appear larger. Also, this is a good shade of lipstick for you." Who probably said this? How do you know?

9. "I'll show you how to get your dog to stop jumping, and lie down. Be sure that everyone in the family uses the commands if you expect your dog to learn." Who probably said this? How do you know?

10. "Everyone, look right at me, smile and stand still." Who probably said this? How do you know?

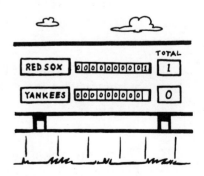

11. "First, the highlights of today's game against the Yankees. Later we'll give you all the American and National League scores, and tell you about the new home run record that was set today." Who probably said this? How do you know?

This page presents suggested answers to the question, "Who . . . ?" on pages 74 to 80. They are in different order than on the pages.

Who?

appliance repair person	puppeteer
astronaut	roofer
dance instructor	sculptor
lumberjack	singer
physical trainer	telephone operator
	weather forecaster

Pg. 77

Who?

actress	fire fighter
bank teller	gardener
barber	pilot
baseball coach	teacher
builder	veterinarian
bus driver	waiter
chef	

Pg. 74

Who?

artist	police officer
cashier	railroad engineer
lifeguard	skydiver
museum guide	symphony conductor
optometrist	web site designer
plumber	

Pg. 78

Who?

author	fisherman
baker	football player
doctor	judge
dry cleaner	librarian
electrician	school principal
farmer	TV announcer

Pg. 75

Who?

circus performer	pilot
dental hygienist	reporter
king	science teacher
magician	telephone service person
model	
parking attendant	

Pg. 79

Who?

butcher	custodian
candidate for congress	director
car salesperson	painter
carpenter	postal worker
clergyman	ship's captain
	taxi driver

Pg. 76

Who?

fashion designer	pianist
make-up artist	shoe salesperson
nurse	soldier
nurseryman	sportscaster
pet trainer	tailor
photographer	

Pg. 80

The Jackson family, Mom, Dad, Rachel, and Lionel have just moved into a new house. They are unpacking their things and putting them away. Each one is talking about something that he or she is putting away, but we do not know what they are talking about!

Use clues that are in the sentences that Mom, Dad, Rachel or Lionel say to figure out **what** they are talking about. Tell how you get your answers!

1.   Mom said, "I'll put this in the freezer right away or it'll melt."
What is she talking about? How do you know?

2.   Rachel said, "I'd better put these on the floor next to my bed so I can put them on after my bath later this evening." What is she talking about? How do you know?

3.   Mom said, "I'll hang all of these up in Lionel's closet. He'll need a clean one tomorrow." What is she talking about? How do you know?

4.   Dad picked up the heavy box and said, "I'll take these right out to the car and put them in the trunk. I sure wouldn't want to be without them if the car breaks down." What is he talking about? How do you know?

5.   Mom said, "I'd better put these here on the table. I might need to write some notes." What is she talking about? How do you know?

6.   Dad put a box on the shelf near the washer and dryer. He said, "We'll need it when we wash our clothes." What is he talking about? How do you know?

7.   Mom said, "I'd like to leave this here on the counter. We might want to take some pictures of our new house." What is she talking about? How do you know?

8.   Dad picked this up from the front porch. He said, "I'm glad we got one of these. Later I'll sit and relax for a while and I can read about what's new in our new neighborhood." What is he talking about? How do you know?

9.   Rachel said, "I'd better hang this up on the wall right here in the kitchen. I can look at it and be reminded when my dentist and my haircut appointments are scheduled." What is she talking about? How do you know?

10. Mom said, "We can put these in the cupboard. It's all cleaned out. We might want to use them for a snack later." What is she talking about? How do you know?

The Jackson family, Mom, Dad, Rachel, and Lionel have just moved into a new house. They are unpacking their things and putting them away. Each one is talking about something that he or she is putting away, but we do not know what they are talking about!

Use clues that are in the sentences that Mom, Dad, Rachel or Lionel say to figure out **what** they are talking about. Tell how you get your answers!

1. "Please put these on the beds upstairs", Mom said to Lionel. "It's supposed to be chilly tonight, and we'll probably need them." What is she talking about? How do you know?

2 Dad said, "I'll put these right here on the counter. Please don't move them. I'll need them to start the car later." What is he talking about? How do you know?

3. Mom said, "I'm going to keep this in my pocket. I might go out later and buy something for us to have for dinner." What is she talking about? How do you know?

4. "We can use this to tie these boxes together when they're empty. Then I can put a bundle of boxes into the recycling bin," Dad said. What is he talking about? How do you know?

5. Rachel said, "I'll put these in the refrigerator so they'll be nice and cold if we get thirsty later." What is she talking about? How do you know?

6. Dad said, "I'll put one of these in each of the lamps so the lamps will work when we turn them on." What is he talking about? How do you know?

7. Dad said, "I'll take this to the back hall. There's some dirt that should be swept up back there." What is he talking about? How do you know?

8. Mom said, "Help me roll this out on the living room floor. Then we can put the furniture just where we want it in the living room." What is she talking about? How do you know?

9. Rachel said, I'll put a roll of these in the kitchen and in the basement so we can wipe up something that might spill." What is she talking about? How do you know?

10. Dad said, "Lionel, put these in the basement on the workbench. We'll be using them next weekend to paint your room." What is he talking about? How do you know?

The Jackson family, Mom, Dad, Rachel, and Lionel have just moved into a new house. They are unpacking their things and putting them away. Each one is talking about something that he or she is putting away, but we do not know what they are talking about!

Use clues that are in the sentences that Mom, Dad, Rachel or Lionel say to figure out **what** they are talking about. Tell how you get your answers!

1. Mom said, "I'd like to put this in my car. I might need to look at one if I need to go somewhere and I'm not sure how to get there." What is she talking about? How do you know?

2. Rachel said, "Look what I found! Can we connect it right away so I can call my friends?" What is she talking about? How do you know?

3. Mom said, "Put these on the counter. We'll need them if we decide to have soup for dinner." What is she talking about? How do you know?

4. Dad said, "I'll put this in the garage for now. Soon I'll need it so I can get up on the roof and look at those loose shingles." What is he talking about? How do you know?

5. Lionel said, "I'll put this on the desk so we can look up someone's number if we need to call them." What is he talking about? How do you know?

6. Rachel said, "I'd better put this up in my room so I can take it to school and put my books and homework in it." What is she talking about? How do you know?

7. Lionel said, "I'll put this bag in the garage. We'll need to use some of this if we grill hamburgers some day." What is he talking about? How do you know?

8. Dad said, "I'll put these in the garage. We'll be using them pretty soon. There are lots of weeds in the garden, and some of those old plants should be dug up." What is he talking about? How do you know?

9. Mom said, "Carefully put this bowl on the counter for now until we find a better place for them. And, you'd better give them some food too." What is she talking about? How do you know?

10. Rachel said, "We'd better put these by the back door. It looks like it might rain pretty soon." What is she talking about? How do you know?

The Jackson family, Mom, Dad, Rachel, and Lionel have just moved into a new house. They are unpacking their things and putting them away. Each one is talking about something that he or she is putting away, but we do not know what they are talking about!

Use clues that are in the sentences that Mom, Dad, Rachel or Lionel say to figure out **what** they are talking about. Tell how you get your answers!

1. Mom said, "We can put these on the shelf in the closet upstairs. We won't need them for a while. We won't be traveling any time soon." What is she talking about? How do you know?

2. Dad said, "I'm going to put these on the desk. I'll have to pay some bills and fill out some papers and put them in the mail soon." What is he talking about? How do you know?

3. Lionel said, "We should put this on the floor in the kitchen. We'll need it when it's time to feed the dog." What is he talking about? How do you know?

4. Mom said, "I'm going to put this in my jewelry box. It's not working now because it needs a new battery. I'll get a new battery and start wearing it soon." What is she talking about? How do you know?

5. Dad said, "Let's put these in the garage. We should put our helmets out there too. Maybe tomorrow we can all take a ride and look around our new neighborhood." What is he talking about? How do you know?

6. Mom said, "I might need this if we decide to open some cans of soup for dinner tonight." What is she talking about? How do you know?

7. Dad said, "I'll put these here on the table. I'll get my hammer and some nails and hang them up on the walls as soon as we decide where we want to put them. It'll be nice to look at them in our new house." What is he talking about? How do you know?

8. Mom said, "I want this in the living room in front of the fireplace. I can't wait 'till it's time to make a fire. I'm going to sit down and put my feet up and enjoy looking at the fire." What is she talking about? How do you know?

9. Lionel said, "I need to put this somewhere that I'll see it and remember to take it with me to practice. I'm going to be playing first base this season, you know!" What is he talking about? How do you know?

The Jackson family, Mom, Dad, Rachel, and Lionel have just moved into a new house. They are unpacking their things and putting them away. Each one is talking about something that he or she is putting away, but we do not know what they are talking about!

Use clues that are in the sentences that Mom, Dad, Rachel or Lionel say to figure out **what** they are talking about. Tell how you get your answers!

1. "Please hand those to me," Mom said, "I have to cut the tags off of these boxes." What is she talking about? How do you know?

2. Dad said, "I'll put this on the back porch for now. I'd better plan to connect it and use it later today. The flowers in the garden look a little dry." What is he talking about? How do you know?

3. Dad said, "I'll put these on the shelf in the garage. I hope that pond out back freezes nice and solid this winter so we can use them." What is he talking about? How do you know?

4. Rachel said, "I'll hang this by the back door so we know where it is when we take the dog for a walk." What is she talking about? How do you know?

5. Mom said, "I'll put this up on the counter in the bathroom upstairs. I noticed that the mirrors are smudged and should be cleaned." What is she talking about? How do you know?

6. Rachel said, "I'll put this on the counter by the sink. Soon I'll go out and pick some flowers from the garden, then I'll fill it with water and put the flowers in." What is she talking about? How do you know?

7. Dad said, "We should probably keep this handy. We're not sure if there's a light that's working in every room. I just put new batteries in it." What is he talking about? How do you know?

8. "I'm glad we found this," Mom said, "I'll need to measure the windows so I know what size curtains to buy." What is she talking about? How do you know?

9. "I'll put these in the bathroom," Rachel said, "we'll need them when we brush our teeth tonight." What is she talking about? How do you know?

10. "Let's put this on the counter," Rachel said. "We can turn it on and listen to some music while we work." Mom said, "Good idea! We can probably hear some news too." What are they talking about? How do you know?

The Jackson family, Mom, Dad, Rachel, and Lionel have just moved into a new house. They are unpacking their things and putting them away. Each one is talking about something that he or she is putting away, but we do not know what they are talking about!

Use clues that are in the sentences that Mom, Dad, Rachel or Lionel say to figure out **what** they are talking about. Tell how you get your answers!

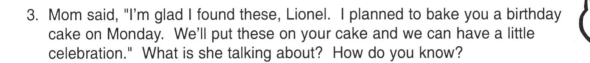
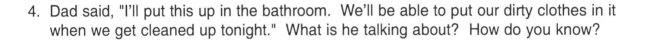

1. Mom said, "I'll put these in the cabinet in the bathroom. If anyone gets a scratch or a cut you'll know where to find them." What is she talking about? How do you know?

2. Rachel asked, "Where can we put these? I suppose we won't be able to play them until we set up the stereo." What is she talking about? How do you know?

3. Mom said, "I'm glad I found these, Lionel. I planned to bake you a birthday cake on Monday. We'll put these on your cake and we can have a little celebration." What is she talking about? How do you know?

4. Dad said, "I'll put this up in the bathroom. We'll be able to put our dirty clothes in it when we get cleaned up tonight." What is he talking about? How do you know?

5. Rachel said, "I'm going to put this on the counter in the bathroom. I hope there's some place to plug it in up there. I want to wash and blow dry my hair later." What is she talking about? How do you know?

6. Lionel said, "Dad, these are yours. You'll be looking for them when you sit down to read that newspaper later." What is he talking about? How do you know?

7. Dad said, "Move everything over on the desk. I'm going to put this down there now. I'll be setting it up pretty soon. There's a lot of information about our new neighborhood that we can probably look up on the internet." What is he talking about? How do you know?

8. Lionel said, "Oh no! Look what I found! I guess I forgot to return these after I finished reading them. I hope I can get them back in time so I don't have to pay a fine." What is he talking about? How do you know?

9. Lionel said, "I'll carry this into the living room so we can plug it in and watch the baseball game later." What is he talking about? How do you know?

This page presents suggested answers to the question, "What . . . ?" on pages 82 to 87. They are in different order than on the pages.

What?

calendar   newspaper
camera   pencils
crackers & cookies   shirts
ice cream   slippers
laundry soap   tools

Pg. 82

What?

blankets   money
broom   paint brushes
drinks   paper towels
keys   rug
light bulbs string

Pg. 83

What?

backpack   ladder
bowls   map
charcoal   phone
garden tools telephone directory
goldfish   umbrellas

Pg. 84

What?

baseball glove   envelopes
bikes   pictures
can opener   suitcases
comfortable chair watch
dog dish

Pg. 85

What?

flashlight scissors
garden hose spray cleaner
ice skates tape measure
leash   tooth brushes
radio   vase

Pg. 86

What?

bandages   glasses
candles   hair dryer
CD's   library books
clothes hamper TV
computer

Pg. 87

Introducing Inference

Read about each of these people and try to figure out **where** they are. Then talk about the clues you found in each sentence that helped you.

1. Ralph put his head back in the chair and opened his mouth wide so his teeth could be seen. Where was Ralph? How do you know?

2. Mike and his friends watched eagerly because the bases were loaded and their favorite player was about to bat. Where were Mike and his friends? How do you know?

3. It was almost time for the animals to be fed. We walked over to see the lions and tigers before their feeding time. Where were we? How do you know?

4. After Eddie finished climbing on the bars, he waited for one of the swings to be free. He thought that after his turn on the swings he would go down the slide. Where was Eddie? How do you know?

5. The captain told all of us to put our life jackets on before we left the dock and got out into harbor. Where were we? How do you know?

6. Dad read the sign that said our exit was coming up in two miles. He got into the right hand lane so he could get off at our exit. Where were we? How do you know?

7. We found everything on our shopping list and put it in our cart. Then we waited in the checkout line. Where were we? How do you know?

8. Kevin put the books that he borrowed last week into his backpack. He put his card in his pocket and walked down the street. He thought about which books he would try to borrow this week. Where was Kevin going? How do you know?

9. Lillian watched the others do their floor and balance beam routines. Then it was her turn to perform on the balance beam. She walked up to the beam, looked at her coach, then began her routine. Where was Lillian? How do you know?

10. Gretchen was eager to ride. She walked past the stalls until she came to Carmel's stall. She opened the gate, then led him out onto the trail. Where were Gretchen and Carmel? How do you know?

Read about each of these people and try to figure out **where** they are. Then talk about the clues you found in each sentence that helped you.

1. The Millers checked in at the desk then took their suitcases up to their room. They hung their clothes, got freshened up, then went out to find a nice place to have dinner. Where were the Millers? How do you know?

2. Joey and Bob looked high up at the peaks. They felt the warm sun on them, yet they could see snow way up at the top. Where were Joey and Bob? How do you know?

3. We looked down at the water on both sides of us as we drove across the lake. We knew that when we got to the other side the cabin would be only a mile down the road. Where were we? How do you know?

4. Dale and his friends shined their flashlights at the dark walls all around them. It felt cool inside and they could hear their voices echo as they talked to each other. Where were Dale and his friends? How do you know?

5. Johnnie waited in the waiting room with his mother. He hoped that the x-ray he'd soon get would show that the bone in his arm was healed and he could get his cast off today. Where were Johnnie and his mother? How do you know?

6. Janice reached inside her bag to find her keys as she walked toward the row where she'd left her car. Where was Janice? How do you know?

7. Mrs. Kim petted her dog and told him "good-bye" as she handed his leash to the attendant. Then she told the man at the desk where she'd be for the weekend and said that she'd be back to pick up her dog on Monday. Where was Mrs. Kim? How do you know?

8. The Klines each took a basket and walked out to pick apples. They stayed together picking apples in the same row of trees. There were many other people out picking apples here today. Where were the Klines? How do you know?

9. While the clerk waited on other customers Michelle looked at the delicious cakes, cookies, rolls and other pastry in the case. She was enjoying the delightful smell coming from the ovens as she decided what she'd buy. Where was Michelle? How do you know?

Read about each of these people and try to figure out **where** they are. Then talk about the clues you found in each sentence that helped you.

1. Pete changed into his swim trunks and went out of the locker room to the pool. He looked around for his friend, Tom, but didn't see him. Pete thought that Tom was probably still working out in the exercise room and would come to the pool when he'd finished his workout. Where were Pete and Tom? How do you know?

2. We fastened our seat belts and took off. Soon after that the flight attendants came down the aisle serving us drinks and snacks. Where were we? How do you know?

3. Bev and her friends picked up their clubs, got a score card and walked out to the course. Someone was teeing off at the first hole, so they had to wait a short time before they could begin their game. Where were Bev and her friends? How do you know?

4. The cows slowly walked out to enjoy some nice fresh grass. They'd be out here all day and come back to the barn at night. Where were the cows? How do you know?

5. Krissy and Beth Ann needed their flashlights to see because it was so dark. They walked around carefully trying not to fall on the rocky floor. They thought that perhaps people might have lived inside here many thousands of years ago. Where were Krissy and Beth Ann? How do you know?

6. Claire listened to her teacher give tonight's homework assignment. Then she put her books inside her backpack. Where was Claire? How do you know?

7. Phil looked at the sign saying "Don't walk." He waited for the sign to say "Walk," then he stepped down off the curb. Where was Phil? How do you know?

8. Melissa drove slowly and carefully because the road was so bumpy. Finally she spotted the cottage with big trees all around it. Where was Melissa? How do you know?

9. Mark climbed up the steps and walked down the aisle to sit in the seat next to his friend. He looked out the window and waved to his mom as they pulled away and drove off to school. Where was Mark? How do you know?

Read about each of these people and try to figure out **where** they are. Then talk about the clues you found in each sentence that helped you.

1. The passengers listened to the Captain talk about the beautiful islands where they would be stopping during the next five days. Then some of them went up on the deck to enjoy the view. Where were these passengers? How do you know?

2. Kim and Jeannie felt the warm sunshine as they lay stretched out on their towels listening to the waves. Where were Kim and Jeannie? How do you know?

3. Polly sold the last ticket to the six o'clock show. She put out the sign that said "SOLD OUT" and went into the lobby. Where was Polly? How do you know?

4. Bud stepped up into the chair and said that he wanted his hair cut shorter than it had been cut the last time. Where was Bud? How do you know?

5. Carol picked up the bag of feed and went out to the barn to feed the chickens. Where was Carol? How do you know?

6. Dad started to drive his car up toward the garage, but he had to get out and move the boys' bicycles which were parked in his way. Where was Dad? How do you know?

7. Lucy and Bill sat at their table and looked at the menu. They decided what they wanted to order and looked around for their waiter. Where were Lucy and Bill? How do you know?

8. Aunt Laura bought tickets for Marcy and Tom and herself and waited until the doors opened. While they waited they looked at the floor plan to find out where different exhibits could be seen. Where were Marcy, Tom and Aunt Laura? How do you know?

9. The Eskimos trudged through the snow looking for a place to build their igloo. When they found the best spot they began to shape hardened snow into large blocks. Where were the Eskimos? How do you know?

Read about each of these people and try to figure out **where** they are. Then talk about the clues you found in each sentence that helped you.

1. The doctor hurried up to the operating room because her patient was ready for surgery. Where was the doctor? How do you know?

2. The astronaut contacted the mission control center to report that the spacecraft had safely entered Mars' orbit. Where was the astronaut? How do you know?

3. The conductor walked down the aisle collecting the tickets from the passengers as they moved along the tracks. Where were the passengers? How do you know?

4. The crowd stood up and cheered as they watched the ball go into the basket and score two points for their team. Where was this crowd? How do you know?

5. Zoe tried to get a taxi to take her from her meeting at the bank back to her office even though her building was only a few blocks away. Where was Zoe? How do you know?

6. George got his bus pass out of his pocket while he stood on the corner waiting. Where was George? How do you know?

7. The Cliftons parked their car and began to set up their tent. Then they found a place where they could build the fire where they'd cook their food. Where were the Cliftons? How do you know?

8. Megan and Toni went inside and walked along looking in the windows of so many stores! They went inside a clothing store and stopped at an ice cream store for a treat. They ate their ice cream on a bench in the center, then went into a sporting goods store to find a gift for Toni's dad. Where were the girls? How do you know?

9. Ben took a tray and looked at the list of lunch specials that he could choose today. Then he walked down the line and made his choices. Where was Ben? How do you know?

Read about each of these people and try to figure out **where** they are. Then talk about the clues you found in each sentence that helped you.

1. Mom sat in the chair and held onto Muffin's leash. Muffin seemed excited as she looked around and saw other dogs and cats with their owners. Soon someone called Mom and Muffin into a room where she put Muffin up on a table and listened to Muffin's heart. Where were Mom and Muffin? How do you know?

2. The sailors anchored their boat down, got out on the shore and started to walk around. They walked for a few minutes then looked around. Everywhere around the land where they stood they could see water. Where were the sailors? How do you know?

3. Russel walked into the lobby and rode the elevator up to the fourth floor. He walked down the hall and knocked on his friend's door, which was marked 4J. Where was Russel? How do you know?

4. Dad and Paul walked down the rows of graves looking at the headstones. Soon they came to the grave where Paul's grandparents were buried. Dad put some flowers down on the grave and he and Paul said a prayer. Where were Dad and Paul? How do you know?

5. Dorey turned her headlights on as she drove through. When she looked ahead she could see light and knew she'd be driving out soon. Where was Dorey? How do you know?

6. Wayne, the mailman, walked up and down the streets putting the people's mail in their mailboxes. Where was Wayne? How do you know?

7. We drove down the dusty road and looked at the tall cactus plants as we passed them. There was no grass growing, only some plants that didn't need much water to survive. We didn't get out of the car to look around because it was too hot outside. Where were we? How do you know?

8. Neil and Cameron held on to their tickets and waited for the line to start moving. They could hardly wait until it was their turn to ride on the Ferris Wheel! They looked around and decided that the next ride they'd go on was the roller coaster. Where were the boys? How do you know?

Introducing Inference

Read about each of these people and try to figure out **where** they are. Then talk about the clues you found in each sentence that helped you.

1. Bruce wanted to deposit some money from his paycheck into his account. He stepped up to the window and handed a deposit slip and a check to the teller. Where was Bruce? How do you know?

2. Frank looked up at the schedule on the wall and bought his ticket. He knew that he had to get to Track Number Two in fifteen minutes so he could board the "four-o'clock" to New York City. Where was Frank? How do you know?

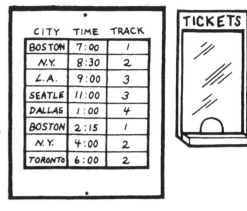

CITY	TIME	TRACK
BOSTON	7:00	1
N.Y.	8:30	2
L.A.	9:00	3
SEATLE	11:00	3
DALLAS	1:00	4
BOSTON	2:15	1
N.Y.	4:00	2
TORONTO	6:00	2

TICKETS

3. Alan raised his racquet. tossed the ball up and hit the ball over the net where it bounced up. Greg hit the ball back over the net. Greg and Alan hit the ball back and forth over the net until Greg hit the ball out of bounds and Alan won the match. Where were the boys? How do you know?

4. Margaret walked along looking at the vegetables and fruits that all the farmers had brought to town to sell. She bought some lettuce and tomatoes and some fresh peaches. Where was Margaret? How do you know?

5. Amy stood at the counter trying to decide whether she wanted a sundae or a cone. There were twenty-five flavors to choose from. Where was Amy? How do you know?

6. We laughed at the clowns as they played silly tricks on each other. Then we watched the amazing show that the trapeze performers put on. Where were we? How do you know?

7. Roy climbed the stairs to the controls. He pulled the switch that shined the beam of light for many miles across the sea. Then he rotated the beam so the ships could safely move into port. Where was Roy? How do you know?

8. The cowboys set out to round up the cattle and bring them in to be branded. After they were branded the cattle would return to the fields to graze. Where were the cowboys and the cattle? How do you know?

Read about each of these people and try to figure out **where** they are. Then talk about the clues you found in each sentence that helped you.

1. Jack jumped up when he heard the bell. He and the others quickly got their boots and heavy waterproof coats and hats on. Then they got into the truck and drove off with the siren sounding and their lights flashing. Where were Jack and the others? How do you know?

2. The judge sat at the bench in front of the room and called for order. Then the lawyer walked over and started to talk to the jury. Where were these people? How do you know?

3. Alex and Jerry walked through the dark rooms thinking that they could hear strange noises and voices. They knew nobody had been inside for many years. Then Alex slowly opened one of the doors of an upstairs bedroom and screamed because he thought he saw a ghost. Where were the boys? How do you know?

4. Mom and Dad walked up and down the rows of cars. They were looking for a car that was big enough for the family, not too expensive and in good condition. If they could find the car they wanted they planned to buy it. Where were Mom and Dad? How do you know?

5. Dixie put her jacket and bag on the bench. She put her ballet slippers on and walked across the large, bright room to do leg warm-ups with the other girls while they waited for class to begin. Where was Dixie? How do you know?

6. Sam went into the building with his dad, then into a room. One of the people behind the long table crossed Dad's name off a list and handed him a ballot. Then Dad took the ballot inside one of the booths and Sam waited outside the booth. When Dad came out he put the ballot into a machine and he and Sam went back home. Where were Dad and Sam? How do you know?

7. Ellie decided to work out on the treadmill before she did her weights. She'd go to the aerobics class after this. Where was Ellie? How do you know?

8. The audience sat perfectly still as the curtain went up. The orchestra members were in position, and the conductor came out on to the stage. He bowed to the audience, then turned around. Where was the audience? How do you know?

Introducing Inference

This page presents suggested answers to the question, "Where . . . ?" on pages 89 to 96. They are in different order than on the pages.

Where?

baseball game	highway
boat	library
dentist's office	playground
grocery store	stable
gymnastics meet	zoo

Pg. 89

Where?

bakery	hotel
boarding kennel	mountain valley
bridge	orchard
cave	parking lot
doctor's office	

Pg. 90

Where?

airplane	golf course
cave	health club
classroom	pasture
country road	school bus
crosswalk	

Pg. 91

Where?

barber shop	movie theatre
beach	Northern Alaska
cruise ship	restaurant
driveway	science museum
farm	

Pg. 92

Where?

basketball game	hospital
bus stop	shopping mall
cafeteria	space ship
campground	train
city center	

Pg. 93

Where?

amusement park	neighborhood
apartment building	tunnel
cemetery	veterinarian's office
desert	
island	

Pg. 94

Where?

bank	ranch
circus	tennis court
ice cream parlor	train station
lighthouse	
produce market	

Pg. 95

Where?

court room	symphony hall
dancing school	used car lot
fire station	voting center
gym	
haunted house	

Pg. 96

Read about these people. Each one has done, is doing or will do something where time is important. Answer the questions. For each question you will have to use ideas about **time**. Information about time is missing from these sentences. Answer the questions and talk about how you figured out your answer.

1. Frank is usually home from football practice in time to eat dinner with his family. On Tuesday Frank stayed at school for an hour after practice to help his coach get equipment ready for Saturday's game. Was Frank early or late for dinner that day? How do you know?

2. The bus usually comes a few minutes after the bells in the church on the corner ring. This morning Phil stood at the bus stop listening to the bells ring as he read the morning paper. Was he early or late for the bus this morning? How do you know?

3. Mom put the cake in the oven to bake. The cake had to bake for 30 minutes. Mom set the timer and went out in the garden to pick some vegetables. She finished picking the vegetables and brought them into the house in about fifteen minutes. Then she went right into the kitchen to check the oven timer. Was this before or after the cake should be ready? How do you know?

4. Margo walks to school. Her friends, Karen and Mia, take the bus. The bus usually arrives at school just as school is about to begin. If Margo gets to school fifteen minutes before school starts, can she visit with Karen and Mia for fifteen minutes before school begins? How do you know?

5. A new grocery store was opening in the neighborhood. The first 100 customers who come to this store would each get a free carton of orange juice. The store opened at nine o'clock. Mr. Hunt hoped to get the free orange juice. He arrived at the store at nine-thirty. There were nearly 100 people in the store when he arrived, and many others who had finished shopping and were going back to their cars. Do you think Mr. Hunt got the free orange juice? How do you know?

6. Barney wanted to watch his cousin, Tim, pitch in his baseball game last Saturday. The game was played for seven innings and started at one o'clock. Tim pitched the first three innings of the game, but another pitcher pitched the last four innings. Barney had arrived at the ball park at twelve-thirty. Do you think he got to see Tim pitch? How do you know?

7. The bankers' meeting started at two o'clock in the afternoon. The president of the bank spoke for the first half hour. Mr. Blake arrived at the meeting at three o'clock. Did he hear the bank president's speech? How do you know?

Introducing Inference

Read about these people. Each one has done, is doing or will do something where time is important. Answer the questions. For each question you will have to use ideas about **time**. Information about time is missing from these sentences. Answer the questions and talk about how you figured out your answer.

1. The mail is usually delivered just before lunchtime. Monday Mom heard the mail carrier out on the porch just after she got home from driving Sid and Emily to school. Was the mail probably early or late that day? How do you know?

2. Russel borrowed three library books for twenty-one days. He finished reading the books and took them back a month later. Do you think Russel had to pay a late fee on his library books? Why do you think so?

3. Skyler, the Nessen's Cocker Spaniel, waits in the driveway and barks at the garbage truck that comes down the street every Monday morning. Neighbors are amazed at how Skyler always seems to know when it's Monday! If the Nessons take Skyler with them on a camping trip for the week-end do you think he'll be back in time to bark at the garbage truck on Monday? Why do you think so?

4. Rodney is going to perform in the talent show tonight. The show begins at seven o'clock. The performers are to be there by six o'clock to get into costumes and make-up. Rodney plans to get his hair cut on the way to the show. Do you think he'll get there in time if he gets his hair cut at five o'clock? What if he gets his hair cut at five-thirty? Why do you think so?

5. Bonnie plans to drive to her cousin's holiday party. Her cousin lives about an hour from Bonnie's house. If Bonnie leaves her house an hour before the party will she be on time for the party? If she leaves her house an hour before the party, but gets a flat tire on the way, do you think she'll be on time? Why do you think so?

6. Dave hurried to his friend Tommy's surprise birthday party. He didn't want to miss the surprise. When he arrived, everyone was glad to see him, especially Tommy. Did Dave get to the party in time to surprise Tommy? How do you know?

7. Jane, Pam and Eve all ran in the track meet. Jane ran faster than Eve, but Pam finished first. Who took the longest time to finish the race? How do you know?

Introducing Inference

Read about these people. Each one has done, is doing or will do something where time is important. Answer the questions. For each question you will have to use ideas about **time**. Information about time is missing from these sentences. Answer the questions and talk about how you figured out your answer.

1. Dad's favorite TV show comes on at nine o'clock on Wednesday nights. Last Wednesday night the President's speech was broadcast from seven o'clock to seven thirty. All programs were pushed back one half hour. What time was Dad's show on last Wednesday? How do you know?

2. The fifth grade students were supposed to turn in their science projects by the end of the first week of February. Austin turned his in on February fifth. Crystal's was turned in on February ninth. Did they turn their projects in on time? How do you know?

3. Don wrote to his friend Jerry and told him about the presents that he and his family had opened that morning. He told Jerry that he was looking forward to coming to visit when school was out next summer. When do you think Don was writing this letter? How do you know?

4. Margie looked through her basket of treats and decided which ones she'd keep and which ones she'd give away. Her costume and mask were still on the chair in her room. When do you think Margie was looking at her candy? How do you know?

5. Sylvia is supposed to leave work at five o'clock. Lately everyone at Sylvia's company was asked to stay after work to help. If Sylvia stays after work she gets paid double. Sylvia earns just enough money to pay for her family's needs at home, food, school expenses and car payments. Last month Sylvia paid for all those things, but she also bought new bicycles for her children. Do you think Sylvia worked late any days last month? How do you know?

6. Fran went to the dentist to have her teeth cleaned and checked the week before her ninth birthday. She was lucky. She had no cavities! The dentist told her to come back for a check-up in six months. The next time Fran saw the dentist was one week after her tenth birthday. Did she do as the dentist asked? How do you know?

7. The Barkers had a special holiday dinner. Before dinner Dad lit the candles in the center of the table. Mom said that these candles would burn for one whole hour, long enough for them to eat their whole dinner. When everyone finished the main course Mom and Dad took the plates out to the kitchen. They took the candles that had finished burning too. Then they brought out the desert. Was Mom right about the candles? How do you know?

Read about each of these events and think about what probably happened. Then read the sentences below each of these paragraphs. Choose two sentences that tell what might have happened. Tell why you chose the sentences that you did and why you did not choose the other one.

1. Tom and Terry watched as Mom took the groceries from the bag and put them away. Everything was put in cupboards or in the refrigerator except a bag of chocolate chip cookies. Mom left this bag of cookies on the counter next to some of her papers. When Dad came home he saw a bag *half* full of chocolate chip cookies on the counter. What could have happened to the rest of the cookies?

   a. Mom and the boys ate the cookies for a snack.

   b. A big storm suddenly struck and blew half the cookies away.

   c. Tom put half of the cookies into a bag and took them outside to share with his friends.

2. When the circus was over, the Bronson Family came out to Row number 32 in the parking lot, the row where Mr. Bronson thought they'd parked. They were very shocked to see that their car was not anywhere in Row 32. What could have happened to the Bronsons' car?

   a. Their car could have been stolen.

   b. Mr. Bronson might have made a mistake about the row number where he'd parked.

   c. A monkey might have escaped from the circus and taken some other monkeys for a ride.

3. Sara walked to school with her friend Jenny one morning. After school that day Sara walked home from school by herself. What could have happened?

   a. Jenny didn't go to school that day.

   b. Jenny stayed after school to help her teacher.

   c. Jenny's mom picked Jenny up from school earlier because she had a doctor's appointment.

4. Pete aimed the remote control at the TV and pushed the power button. The TV didn't go on. What could have happened?

   a. Someone had unplugged the TV.

   b. The elcetric power was off all over Pete's house.

   c. Tim couldn't find the remote control.

Read about each of these events and think about what probably happened. Then read the sentences below each of these paragraphs. Choose two sentences that tell what might have happened. Tell why you chose the sentences that you did and why you did not choose the other one.

1. Dana's dad read the announcement of today's parade in the morning paper. Dana was proud that he'd be marching in the parade. He put on his band uniform, picked up his trumpet and walked to the school yard where the parade marchers were supposed to meet. When he got there, he saw no other marchers. What could have gone wrong?

    a. Dana was too early and no one else had arrived yet.

    b. The parade had taken place the day before and Dana had missed it.

    c. The meeting place for the parade marchers had been changed and Dana didn't know about this change.

2. Mom set a bag of groceries on the front seat of the car while she scraped some ice from the car windows. She quickly drove home and brought the groceries into the house. Teddy searched through the grocery bag looking for the ice cream he'd asked Mom to buy. He was disappointed to find no ice cream in the bag. What could have happened?

    a. The ice cream had melted in the hot car.

    b. Mom had not bought the ice cream

    c. Mom had bought two bags of groceries, and the ice cream was in the other bag.

3. Ozzie finished his math homework paper and put it on his desk. The next day he looked in his math book for his math homework but it wasn't there. What could have happened?

    a. Ozzie put the math homework paper into his science book by mistake.

    b. Ozzie left his homework paper on his desk.

    c. Ozzie didn't do his math homework because he didn't understand how.

4. Roscoe, the dog, stays in the hall in back of the house behind the kitchen while Mr. and Mrs. Charles are at work and Patsy Charles is at school. When Patsy got home from school one day Roscoe wasn't in the hall. He was sitting on the couch in the living room. What could have happened?

    a. Mr. or Mrs Charles got home before Patsy and let Roscoe out of the back hall and into the house.

    b. Roscoe found a key and unlocked the kitchen door and let himself in.

    c. No one had closed and locked the kitchen door that day, and Roscoe had been inside the house all day.

Read about each of these events and think about what probably happened. Then read the sentences below each of these paragraphs. Choose two sentences that tell what might have happened. Tell why you chose the sentences that you did and why you did not choose the other one.

1. Roger gets the mail from his mailbox everyday when he comes home from work. One day Roger checked his mailbox and there was no mail. What could have happened?

   a. No one had sent Roger any mail.

   b. The mailbox and all the mail inside had blown away during a wind storm earlier that day.

   c. Roger had gotten home from work early that day, and the mail had not been delivered yet.

2. When the Kellys came home from their two week summer vacation they saw that the tree in their front yard had almost no leaves on it. What could have happened?

   a. There had been a big wind storm and all the leaves had blown off.

   b. The tree had a disease that caused the leaves to fall off.

   c. There had been a big snow storm while they were gone, and the freezing cold weather caused the leaves to fall off.

3. Mom heard the phone ringing and answered it. She said, "Hello," but heard only the dial tone, no one answered her. What could have happened?

   a. The phone was dead because the phone wires had blown down in a storm.

   b. Someone called, then hung up just before Mom answered the phone.

   c. Someone called, but Mom took too long to answer the phone and the caller hung up.

4. Dad and little Henry came home and no one else was home. Henry went to play with his favorite toy, a little toy train, but the train was broken. Henry started to cry. He had been playing with the toy train before he went out with Dad, and it was okay then. What could have happened?

   a. Henry's older sister and her friends might have broken the train while Henry and Dad were gone.

   b. Mom might have dropped and broken the train when she was cleaning up.

   c. Henry couldn't find his toy train.

Read about each of these events and think about what probably happened. Then read the sentences below each of these paragraphs. Choose two sentences that tell what might have happened. Tell why you chose the sentences that you did and why you did not choose the other one.

1. Today is Jessica's birthday. When she got up this morning she saw a beautifully wrapped present on the dining room table. It was a long, tall rectangular box about as big as a loaf of bread. Jessica thought about the present all day and wondered what it could be. What could it be?

    a. It was a new purse.

    b. It was a basketball.

    c. It was a new pair of shoes.

2. Andre agreed to take care of his next door neighbors' dog, Rascal, for a week while his neighbors were on vacation. The first six days of the week Andre went next door, in the morning, afternoon and evening, unlocked the door, and Rascal greeted him. On the seventh day, Andre went next door in the morning and Rascal greeted him, but in the afternoon, Rascal didn't greet Andre at the door! What could have happened?

    a. Andre's neighbors might have gotten home earlier than they thought and took Rascal somewhere.

    b. Rascal was sound asleep in another part of the house and didn't hear Andre.

    c. Rascal decided to play a trick on Andre. He hid in the closet and locked the door from the inside.

3. Jill was all ready to go to work. She got her car keys, unlocked the door and got in. She put the key into the ignition and turned it. When she turned the key the car made a strange noise but would not start. What could have happened?

    a. The car battery was dead.

    b. Jill had gotten into someone else's car.

    c. The car had run out of gas.

4. Marshall was driving around trying to find his new doctor's office downtown. He'd gotten directions and written down the address when he made the appointment yesterday, yet he could not find the office. What could have happened?

    a. Marshall might have written the directions and address incorrectly.

    b. Marshall's appointment was really last week.

    c. Marshall might have been looking for the doctor's office on the wrong street.

Read about each of these events and think about what probably happened. Then read the sentences below each of these paragraphs. Choose two sentences that tell what might have happened. Tell why you chose the sentences that you did and why you did not choose the other one.

1. Jackie walked up the street as usual on her way home from school. When she walked into the house she smelled burnt food. What could have caused this smell?

    a. Jackie's neighbor two doors away burned some potatoes earlier that day.

    b. Jackie's brother had gotten home a little while ago and burned a piece of toast.

    c. Mom had baked a cake earlier and some of the batter dripped onto the bottom of the oven and burned.

2. When Iris walked to school this morning it was windy, rainy and cold. She wore her winter jacket and her mittens. After school Iris put her warm jacket and mittens on and started to walk back home. On the way home she noticed that she was uncomfortably warm. What could have happened during the day?

    a. The wind and rain had stopped and this made it feel warmer than before.

    b. Someone accidentally turned on the furnace outside and heated up the whole town.

    c. The rain stopped and the sun came out and this made the temperature warmer.

3. Before the baseball game began last Sunday the players from each team came onto the field. When Mike came out everyone stood up and cheered very loud. Why do you think this happened?

    a. This was the last game Mike would play before he retired from baseball.

    b. Mike had broken the record for the most base hits by a player in the history of the team.

    c. Mike had just hit a home run and the score was now tied.

4. Aaron put his library books on the counter marked "Returns." Then he chose three more books to take home to read. When he went to check out these books he couldn't find his library card. What could have happened?

    a. Aaron had left his library card inside one of the books that was returned.

    b. Aaron wouldn't be old enough to get a library card until next year.

    c. Aaron forgot to bring his card to the library with him.

Read about each of these events and think about what probably happened. Then read the sentences below each of these paragraphs. Choose two sentences that tell what might have happened. Tell why you chose the sentences that you did and why you did not choose the other one.

1. Paul poured a glass of milk and took a sip. The milk tasted a little sour, as though it was spoiled. What could have happened?

   a. Someone had put sugar in the milk.

   b. Someone had left the milk out all day, and it spoiled because it should have been refrigerated.

   c. The milk spoiled because it was too old.

2. Carrie and Peter were the only students running for class president. The students went to the gym, got their ballots, and voted for either Peter or Carrie. Later that day the principal announced that Carrie had won the election and would be the new class president! Why do you suppose Carrie won the election?

   a. Carrie had gotten more votes than Peter.

   b. Peter had gotten almost as many votes as Carrie, but not quite as many.

   c. Peter had decided not to run for president, and his name was not on the ballot.

3. Marissa got off the plane, picked up her suitcase at the airport and took a cab to her hotel. In her hotel room she planned to get ready for her business meeting tomorrow morning. She opened her suitcase and was shocked to find a beautiful sweater that she'd never seen before right on top! What could have happened?

   a. A magician on the plane could have done a magic trick and turned her nightgown into a beautiful sweater.

   b. Marissa picked up someone else's suitcase at the airport by mistake thinking it was hers.

   c. Marissa's husband might have surprised her with a new sweater, and put it into her suitcase when she wasn't looking.

4. Ada planned to have flowers, beans and tomatoes growing in her garden last Summer. In May she planted the seeds for her flowers and vegetables. Ada was disappointed. By late Summer she had flowers growing in her garden, but no vegetables. What could have happened?

   a. Temperatures in May might have been too cold for the seeds to develop.

   b. Animals might have eaten the vegetables from Ada's garden.

   c. Ada decided to dig up her garden and put in a swimming pool and did not plant anything last Spring.

Read about each of these events and think about what probably happened. Then read the sentences below each of these paragraphs. Choose two sentences that tell what might have happened. Tell why you chose the sentences that you did and why you did not choose the other one.

1. Sylvia wrote the time and date of her haircut appointment. When she got to the hair salon, she was told that she didn't have an appointment that day. What could have happened?

    a. Sylvia had written her appointment date and time incorrectly.

    b. Sylvia went to the salon on the wrong day.

    c. The salon had moved to a new location.

2. Shelly had been on time for school every day this year. One day near the end of the school year she arrived at school late. She went to the office and talked to the school secretary. Why could Shelly have been late that morning?

    a. She missed the bus and her mother had to drive her.

    b. She walked to school, and fell down on the way and hurt her knee so she had to walk very slowly.

    c. It was the first day of school and Shelly didn't know where the school was.

3. Ruthie and her friend Sue went to a movie at a large theater where there was a choice of four movies. One of the movies was about outer space, another about the jungle, one was a mystery and the other was a musical. Ruthie wanted to see the movie about the jungle and Sue wanted to see the musical. The girls ended up seeing the movie about outer space. What could have happened?

    a. The theatre was closed.

    b. The girls thought it would be fair to choose a movie that was different from either one of their favorites.

    c. The tickets were sold out for all but the outer space movie.

4. Laurie was flying her kite as she ran along the beach. Her kite was up high in the sky and she could see it as she ran. Suddenly Laurie could not see her kite any longer. What could have happened?

    a. Laurie's kite string might have broken and the kite blew away.

    b. The wind might have stopped and no longer lifted the kite up in the air and the kite fell to the ground.

    c. A huge fish jumped up out of the water and ate the kite.

Read about each of these events and think about what probably happened. Then read the sentences below each of these paragraphs. Choose two sentences that tell what might have happened. Tell why you chose the sentences that you did and why you did not choose the other one.

1. Mr. Carney drove past Mapledale Elementary, his son's school this morning. He noticed something unusual. All the students from Mapledale were standing outside the building lined up by classroom. What could have been happening at Mapledale Elementary this morning?

   a. The students at Mapledale Elementary were having a fire drill.

   b. The principal might have thought that there was a serious problem in the school and that the children should evacuate the building.

   c. There was no school at Mapledale Elementary today.

2. Fran was doing her regular grocery shopping at her favorite grocery store. When she went to the cereal aisle to buy her family's favorite cereal, Monster Puffs, there was an empty space on the shelf where this cereal should be. What might have happened to Monster Puffs Cereal?

   a. Someone had poured all the Monster Puffs onto a big pile on the shelf and threw the boxes down on the floor.

   b. The manager of this store decided that she would no longer sell Monster Puffs Cereal, and some other cereal would soon be put in this space.

   c. This week's order of Monster Puffs Cereal had not come in yet, and would arrive later that day.

3. Ms. Randolph, the principal, announced that today there would be no gym classes at school today. What could have happened that caused Ms. Randolph to make this announcement?

   a. The gym was all set up for the school's annual book fair, and there was no space for gym classes to be held today.

   b. The gym teacher had called in sick that morning and wouldn't be in school today.

   c. The music teacher had called in sick and wouldn't be in school today.

4. Seymour got into his car and turned the key to start it up. The key turned just as it always did when the car was started, but there was no sound from the car's engine. He had driven the car yesterday and it had been just fine. What could have happened to Seymour's car that night?

   a. The car's battery had died overnight so the car couldn't start.

   b. Sheldon was using the wrong key.

   c. The car's starter was worn out and had just stopped working so the car couldn't get started.

Read about each of these events and think about what probably happened. Then read the sentences below each of these paragraphs. Choose two sentences that tell what might have happened. Tell why you chose the sentences that you did and why you did not choose the other one.

1. Mom took David to the pumpkin farm so he could choose a pumpkin for his Halloween jack-o'-lantern. David chose a big round pumpkin that was just right for a happy or a scary face. On Halloween there was no jack-o'-lantern in David's front window. What could have happened?

   a. Mom and David didn't have time to carve the jack-o'-lantern so the pumpkin was still in the kitchen.

   b. They decided to put the scary-faced jack-o'-lantern out on the porch.

   c. It was raining at the pumpkin farm so David didn't get a pumpkin for Halloween this year.

2. Phyllis came home to her apartment from a long day at work. She unlocked her door, stepped inside and flipped on the light switch by the door. However, it was still dark. She looked around and saw that her neighbors in her apartment building had lights in their apartments. What could have happened?

   a. The bulb in that lamp was burned out.

   b. Lightning had struck during the day and the electric power was out all over the area.

   c. That lamp was not plugged in.

3. Darby woke up and saw the sun shining bright outside. She remembered the weather forecaster saying that it would be warm. She decided to wear a cool sleeveless dress to work. When she stepped outside, however, she was cold even though the sun was still shining. What could have happened?

   a. It was cool in the morning but the temperature would rise as the day went on.

   b. It was winter time and she shouldn't have expected the weather to be warm.

   c. The weather forecaster was not aware of a cool front moving in.

4. Bud was planning to travel by bus from Seattle, Washington to San Diego, California. He found out a bus trip would take over two days. This seemed like a long time. Bud arrived in San Diego the next day. What could have happened?

   a. Bud decided to drive to San Diego instead of taking the bus.

   b. Bud went on a bus from a different bus company.

   c. Bud decided to take a plane to San Diego.

Read about each of these events and think about what probably happened. Then read the sentences below each of these paragraphs. Choose two sentences that tell what might have happened. Tell why you chose the sentences that you did and why you did not choose the other one.

1. Carla bought a tool kit for her friend Anita for her birthday. It was very heavy and Carla couldn't carry it over to Anita's house. She talked to her dad about the problem and he said he would help. The present arrived at Anita's house in time for the party. What could have happened?

    a. Carla's dad drove her to Anita's party and they took the present in the car.

    b. Carla carried the present to Anita's house in a shopping bag.

    c. Dad dropped Anita's present off on his way to work on the morning of the party.

2. Krista found the CD she wanted in the music store. She could hardly wait to get home so she could play it. She took it to the cashier and waited in line to pay for it. However, Krista left the music store without the CD. What could have happened?

    a. The CD was damaged and there was not another one in stock in the store.

    b. While Krista was in line she realized that she didn't have any money with her.

    c. Krista doesn't have a CD player.

3. Sophie held her balloon for a while, then she let the string go. She watched it go up toward the sky for a while, then she couldn't see the balloon anymore. What could have happened?

    a. The balloon popped because it touched something sharp high on a building.

    b. The balloon fell to the ground because it was too heavy.

    c. The balloon went up so far that it became too tiny to see from the ground.

4. Courtney took a peach from the grocery bag on the table. She thought the peach would be good to eat, but when she bit into it she was disappointed. What could have been wrong?

    a. The peach was not ripe enough to eat. It was still too hard.

    b. The peach was rotten in some places.

    c. She dropped the peach while she was taking it out of the bag and decided not to try it.